Women and Work in Mexico's Maquiladoras

Women and Work in Mexico's Maquiladoras

Altha J. Cravey

ROWMAN & LITTLEFIELD PUBLISHERS, INC.
Lanham • Boulder • New York • Oxford

ROWMAN & LITTLEFIELD PUBLISHERS, INC.

Published in the United States of America
by Rowman & Littlefield Publishers, Inc.
4720 Boston Way, Lanham, Maryland 20706

12 Hid's Copse Road
Cumnor Hill, Oxford OX2 9JJ, England

British Library Cataloguing in Publication Information Available

Library of Congress Cataloging-in-Publication Data

Cravey, Altha J., 1952-
    Women and work in Mexico's maquiladoras / Altha J. Cravey.
       p. cm.
    Includes bibliographical references and index.
    ISBN 0-8476-8885-2 (cloth : alk. paper). — ISBN 0-8476-8886-0 (pbk. : alk.
paper)
    1. Women offshore assembly industry workers — Mexico. 2. Industrial
policy — Mexico. 3. Work and family — Mexico.
HD6073.0332M4954 1998
331.4'87'0972 — dc21   98-36864
                                                 CIP

Printed in the United States of America

♾️[TM] The paper used in this publication meets the minimum requirements of
American National Standard for Information Sciences — Permanence of Paper for
Printed Library Materials, ANSI Z39.48-1984.

For my parents,

Margaret Eileen and Gerald Tyson Cravey

Contents

Figures and Tables

Figures

Tables

Acknowledgments

I accumulated many debts in the research and writing of this book. It is my pleasure to thank some of the people who provided assistance, support, or encouragement along the way. I am particularly grateful to the countless people in Mexico who offered guidance and contributed their thoughts and criticisms. Likewise I am deeply indebted to the University of Iowa for awarding me a generous Iowa Fellowship, which subsidized the field research as well as my graduate education. During my years at the University of Iowa, I had a number of wonderful advisers. Rebecca Roberts, David Reynolds, Charles Hale and Florence Babb were among them. The gentleness, patience, and wisdom of my principal adviser, Abdi Samatar, were so vast that they easily sustained me throughout my tenure as a graduate student.

Many others contributed to my interest in exploring ideas about gender, work, global politics, and international development. Jan Monk, Andrew Kirby, William Thiesenhusen, and Frederick Bein were especially influential. Other intellectual debts have become quite personal over the years. I have been fortunate to share ideas at crucial moments with Larry Knopp and Gail Hollander.

At the University of North Carolina at Chapel Hill I would like to thank my chair Leo Zonn for maintaining a space for intellectual growth in the geography department. Likewise, the Institute for Latin American Studies at the University of North Carolina has been an immensely supportive organization. I feel fortunate indeed to be part of this network. During my search for a publisher for this manuscript, Lars Schoultz offered the kind of advice that is so great it is impossible to calculate. Barbara Harris's unrelenting enthusiasm during this process is also much appreciated. A smaller and more intimate local group deserves special acknowledgment. The members of my writing group, Jan Bardsley, Joanne Hershfield, and Megan Matchinske, have been the source of continuing inspiration and support.

Portions of two chapters were published in *Economic Geographer* and in *Organizing the Landscape*, University of Minnesota Press. I am grateful to the editors, Richard Peet and Andrew Herod, and their reviewers for helping to sharpen my argument and my prose. Furthermore, I appreciate the willingness of those organizations to grant permission to reprint sections of those articles. Production assistance for the book was cheerfully contributed by G. R. Dobbs, who produced the maps, and Carolyn Coffay.

Kindness is especially sweet during intense periods of field work. Teresa Leal, Martha Monroy, Jill Zapien, Francisco Lara at the Colegio de la Frontera Norte, Catalina Denman of Hermosillo, and the family of Alfredo Pliego Aldana in Ciudad Madero were particularly helpful in different stages of the research.

Thanks are long overdue to my many sisters and brothers in the construction industry, especially to members of the International Brotherhood of Electrical Workers local #481 in Indianapolis, Indiana, who were with me when I first began to think about and question the way in which gender becomes attached to specific occupations and how this process get embedded in particular places. While intensely interested in this subject in earlier days, I did not then suspect that I would someday write books on the subject. I imagine that many of my former colleagues would be surprised to see this as well.

Finally, I would like to thank members of my family for their confidence and support. My sister, Georgia Cravey, and my parents have puzzled over the idiosyncrasies of the academic path I chose, but never tried to dissuade or discourage me. To the contrary, they have been crucial to the success of my work. My brother-in-law and my mother-in-law likewise have been a source of strength. Most significantly of all, I am grateful to Jim for his sacrifices, which are reflected in each of the following pages.

1

Introduction

Does the internationalization of labor markets in the late twentieth century allow one to generalize about the changing nature of work? Will increasing competition between large pools of unemployed in the Third World and workers in advanced capitalist economies tend to degrade but equalize the conditions of work? If so, does the proliferation of jobs in export industries of the Third World offer a glimpse of our collective future? What theoretical and practical strategies can be derived from the scrutiny of working conditions in these industries?

This study examines the gendered nature of social reproduction and export production in the foreign-owned assembly plants of northern Mexico.[1] Commonly referred to as maquiladoras, these factories flourished after a 1965 Mexican program began to offer incentives to corporations willing to locate manufacturing plants at the U.S.-Mexico border. This research moves between an analysis of households, classes, and the state in order to contrast the maquiladora factory regime with its historical antecedent.[2] The central goal is to understand the intersection of class and gender dynamics in the radical transformation of Mexican industrial strategy, from an ambitious state-led import substitution emphasis to a neoliberal export-orientation based on transnational investment.[3]

The research draws upon two distinct urban case studies. The first to be presented is Ciudad Madero, Tamaulipas, which represents the earlier state-led period of industrial growth between 1930 and 1976. The social history and geography of this case is then contrasted with the more recent maquiladora factory regime in Nogales, Sonora. These case studies form the basis of my analysis of the pattern and evolution of

Mexican industrialization and include worker interviews at each site. The contrast is drawn at its most extreme in order to highlight the dynamics of the transition and the consequences of the maquiladora factory regime for workers.

I argue that gender analysis is essential for understanding the industrial transition in Mexico and the mode of capital accumulation that it supports. The evidence suggests that gender may be an important way of understanding Third World economic development more generally. Curiously, gender is absent in the debate to which it might be most relevant–those discussions concerning the impetus behind the phenomenal growth rates of the newly industrializing countries (NICs). Although the labor force in many of the most dynamic sectors of East Asian NICs are overwhelmingly female, this fact, when recognized, is considered unproblematic by many development scholars. The mechanisms that have propelled women into the workforce are unexamined. The processes of exploitation based on gender, whether they be subsumed class processes or otherwise, remain obscured. The restructuring of households and the flexibility of the very notion of maleness and femaleness have been ignored.

By delving beneath the surface of Mexico's shift to export production, this research hopes to contribute to issues of immediate and practical significance. The economic survival of large segments of the border region's population depends on the maquiladora industry. For more than a decade, maquiladora export-assembly has been the fastest growing sector of the economy, surpassing the rates of expansion of oil production and tourism. The industry had moved ahead of other sources of revenue in the 1990s, becoming the largest source of foreign exchange. The quality of employment in this crucial industry and the implications of deeper social changes that accompany production changes will impact Mexican life for many years. The maquiladora factory regime became the model for the 1994 neoliberal North American Free Trade Agreement (NAFTA), and thus has broader relevance for working people throughout the North American continent.

This research also is relevant to the theoretical issue of the relationship of space and social theory. The factory regime that replaced the previous state-led model of industrialization emerged in a distinct pattern, remote from the existing industrial agglomerations. This displacement, although hardly thought out, was fortuitous from the perspective of capital accumulation, because it facilitated the imposition of new norms of employment–with minimal resistance.

Industrialization and the Developmentalist State

Industrialization has long been recognized as fundamental to development because growth in the industrial sector can provide jobs as well as improve technical capacity in the agricultural and service sectors. However, the scholarly debate has focused on the necessary conditions for industrialization as well as its prospects. Trying to explain the spatial patterning of industrialization and diverse historical experiences, many began to assert the importance of strategic choices faced by the state sector within particular countries. A "statist" tradition within development theory has recognized that internal class relations are linked to international economic relations through the state.

Peter Evans' study of industrialization in Brazil was one of the first case studies to note the positive effect of a strong state policy. He suggested that "dependent development" in Brazil was encouraged by an authoritarian military state that provided state subsidies, organized state-owned enterprises, and promoted corporate alliances. Evans labeled the coordination of local and international capitalists with the Brazilian state a "triple alliance" (Evans 1979).

The NICs of East Asia, particularly South Korea and Taiwan, have provoked increased debate about the role of the state in economic development. The NICs' unprecedented rates of economic growth in the 1960s and 1970s led the international financial community to point to these states, as well as Hong Kong and Singapore, as models for the industrialization of the entire Third World. The World Bank and the International Monetary Fund argue that other countries can achieve similar rates of growth by opening their domestic markets and orienting their production to export markets.

In contrast, recent research has revealed that *state* manipulation of the market has been fundamental in fostering industrialization. The state seems to have taken the superior position in the East Asian "triple alliances" by strict management of foreign as well as domestic capital. In South Korea, Amsden calls this "getting the prices wrong" (Amsden 1990). How was this accomplished?

In South Korea, closely monitored state subsidies were used to promote export-oriented manufacturing. Export targets were imposed on all firms that received subsidies, price controls were negotiated annually, banks were owned or controlled by the state, and capital flight was controlled (Amsden 1990). In Taiwan, the state coupled its control of the financial system with state or party-owned firms in strategic industrial sectors such as petroleum and communications. Fully one-third of all fixed investments in the 1970s were in state enterprises (Jenkins 1991b). A small group of private entrepreneurs who were well connected to the Kuomintang party were able to build industrial capacity and produce goods for rapidly expanding global markets.

In addition to these financial strategies, NIC success also was due to the "relative autonomy" of the Asian states. The Japanese colonial legacy left behind a strong administrative infrastructure in Taiwan as well as in South Korea. In contrast to Latin American states, Asian NICs were free from any significant industrial bourgeoisie and, after land reforms in the 1950s, were relatively free from the demands of a landed aristocracy (Gold 1986; Evans 1987). The combination of this weakness of internal classes with a strategic geopolitical position allowed Taiwan and South Korea to insulate the state bureaucracy against outside challenges. Both these bureaucracies were then capable of enforcing finely tuned policies that could target particular sectors and even particular firms within sectors (Deyo 1987). State policies also have been instrumental in supplying cheap labor for the export-oriented industries of the Asian NICs. Both the political exclusion of labor, through labor union control and the prohibition of strikes, and low state expenditures on social welfare have contributed to the economic success of Asian NICs.

This increased attention to the role of the state in industrialization has begun to detail for us *how* industrialization has been nurtured by these developmentalist states. However, with their attention focused on macro-scale processes, most of these theorists have neglected the *quality* of development, especially the quality of the jobs associated with this type of growth. Michael Burawoy's concept of factory regimes provides a way to understand this vital link (Burawoy 1985).

The argument advanced by Burawoy goes to the heart of the *quality* issue through a historical examination of the extent to which workers in advanced capitalist countries have depended on their jobs for survival. Complete dependence characterized a period of "market despotism" in which workers, because they possessed no other means of subsistence, were compelled to sell their labor for a wage. Capitalist firms, competing for their own survival, devised ways of controlling workers through the organization of the labor process (Braverman 1974; Burawoy 1985). By simultaneously producing and obscuring surplus value, economic coercion was coupled with ideological and political violence. The process of worker subordination was oiled by the existence of large reservoirs of unemployed workers that could be drawn upon to replace less productive workers and malcontents. The state was not involved in the regulation of capitalist production; it did not monitor the production process (Burawoy 1985).

Massive state intervention transformed a period of "market despotism" into a period of "hegemonic regimes," and workers were able to meet some of their needs outside of the market, through state provision. Social insurance legislation and labor legislation guaranteed a minimal standard of living in the industrialized countries. At the same time, states began to recognize labor unions and to regulate the labor process. Although hegemonic regimes differed from country to country according to the degree and nature of state intervention, all hegemonic regimes mitigated the complete coercion of workers with a degree of consent (Burawoy 1985).

Hegemonic Despotism

Burawoy suggests that the internationalization of capital is now producing a qualitatively different phase which he labels "hegemonic despotism." New forms of coercion bind social reproduction to the production process so that communities, regions, and nation-states are alert and responsive to the increased mobility of capital. State intervention (e.g., tax holidays and other concessions to capital) helps to attract and retain capital investment in particular localities and regions. States also are moving away from social provision. Like the two preceding phases, this is producing a variety of factory regimes. Its typical form in the Third World is seen in those industries that employ single young women to assemble consumer goods in export-processing zones.

If Burawoy is correct, an examination of these export processing zones, such as the Mexican maquiladora, could help delineate the changing nature of work. The politics of production in the maquiladora can be examined through the concept of the "factory regime," linking the apparatus of production regulation to the organization of the labor process. The first question in this examination will be: *How is the labor process being restructured?* This question has invigorated existing debates on Third World industrialization by shifting the perspective to the standpoint of the workers themselves (Munck 1988; Wood 1989).

The question cannot be addressed in isolation, because the labor process is premised on the health and vitality of the worker. "Social reproduction," that is, the daily and generational restoration of the workers, must be examined as well. Burawoy's periodization of capitalism rests upon state intervention in social reproduction, followed by a withdrawal from involvement in social reproduction. His thesis leads us to expect that the new industrial "hegemonic regimes" of the Third World will be actively dismantling state programs of social provision as well as protective labor regulations.

In the same way that the state has provided some social requisites, the household and the family have clearly done the same. The tasks of social reproduction (such as the daily preparation of food and the care and socialization of children) are essential to wage labor production. The extent of self-provisioning within the household/family has changed through time, and feminist theorists have argued that these transformations are connected to changes in the relations of production (Benería and Sen 1982; Laslett and Brenner 1989). The question must be: *How is the reorganization of production influencing and being influenced by the reorganization of the work of social reproduction?* This question suggests that the transfer of social reproductive tasks among the institutions of the household, the market, and the state, as well as the gendered division of labor within these institutions, must be carefully considered and grounded in a historical understanding of production and reproduction (Abramovitz 1988; Laslett and Brenner 1989). Rephrasing the question in this way, gender analysis becomes relevant to the debates about Third World industrialization.

Gender Analysis

Scholars have used gender analysis to examine the production/reproduction dialectic in Third World export processing zones. There are at least 107 such industrial zones in fifty-one countries which produce manufactured goods for export. There is general agreement that the preferred labor force in these zones is female, very young, and with little or no previous work experience. Furthermore, these women are usually migrants from a "supporting agricultural region." The growth of the export industrial sector is generally an explicit state policy designed to improve the country's international economic position. To pursue this developmental goal, states subsidize industrial sectors, ensure labor tranquility through repressive tactics, and relax environmental and labor regulations (Safa 1981; 1990; Chapkis and Enloe 1983; Tiano 1987). As a result, the workers endure unhealthy and unsafe working conditions to earn salaries that are inadequate for supporting themselves and their families (Wolf 1990). High turnover rates in the factories (often due to work related disabilities) and high rates of unemployment in the urban area guarantee the average worker only a few years of income before she is replaced (Ward 1990). Statistical surveys tell us that the average Mexican worker spends only three years in maquiladora employment (Carrillo 1985, 19).

Labor discipline is enforced in part through the cultivation of rigid gender roles. One technique, which takes advantage of existing gender hierarchies, is the use of male floor managers alongside female line workers. Foreign gender hierarchies are superimposed on existing ones when cosmetic vendors are invited inside the factories by the owner to promote Western ideals of beauty and femininity (Grossman 1979; Fernández-Kelly 1983a; Fuentes and Ehrenreich 1983; Ong 1987). Sexual harassment of females by male managers is another technique of labor discipline, which in many cases may extend beyond working hours. For instance, Peña reports that in Mexican maquiladoras, women who socialize with their supervisors (i.e., waged concubines) are rewarded, while those who refuse are ostracized or threatened with termination (Peña 1987).

Families, households, and individuals have adopted a variety of different coping strategies in the face of these adverse conditions. Families may alter their composition by inviting others into the household, or they may change their pattern of marriage and child-bearing. In Taiwan and Hong Kong, Salaff found that working daughters have chosen to delay marriage in order to "repay" their parents for their upbringing by contributing several years of earnings from their manufacturing jobs (Salaff 1981; 1990). In other contexts, households have increased total income by expanding to include unrelated individuals. In many cases, families trim expenses by living in makeshift housing without plumbing or electricity. Self-provisioning or "informal" economic activity by some household members is often essential to family survival (Kamel 1990). In the Philippines and Thailand, Ong has argued that many women who have lost their jobs in the factories turn to the thriving prostitution industry as a last resort (Ong 1985).

It is interesting to consider states and their planning efforts in light of these gender concerns. Some feminist theory suggests that the public sector offers both possibilities and contradictions for gender equity. The spatiality of states complicates this notion. As they appropriate and demarcate territory, states take shape at the intersection of international relationships and domestic class/race/gender processes. These social webs of relationships may cross the sovereign territorial boundaries of states and are in turn subject to state regulation. The way in which states conjoin these external and internal social processes (or not) influences the nature of a particular state. In this process, states bend and compress the lines of international power into peculiar and diverse spatial forms.

What concepts do we need to be able to examine the state in gendered terms? First, gender must be understood as a set of culturally defined traits labeled masculinity and femininity. It is a social concept,
not a physiological one. Gender differences are thus highly variable in
different historical and geographical contexts. The individual's experience of gender also will be influenced by his class and racial/ethnic
position. A technique used in the geography literature for dealing with
this variation is the concept of a gender contract, which describes the
balance of power that is worked out between men and women in particular places (Duncan 1994, 1186).

Gender contracts within a locality or a region reflect deeply embedded ideas about masculinity and femininity, while, at the level of
the nation-state, gender contracts are institutionalized in official policies and practices (Connell 1994; Duncan 1994; Walby 1994; Kofman
1996). The national gender contract, also known as gender regime, might
be understood as the product of multiple social struggles occurring at a
variety of sites and at many geographical scales. Place, place-based resources, and place-based alliances affect the outcome of these contests.
The resulting geographical patterns of uneven power relationships
influence and are influenced by local struggles. The interaction and
aggregation of small-scale, local contests continually produce new geographical patterns. Negotiations over the gendered balance of power
within the state are thus understood as dynamically linked to a wider
gender order (Connell 1994). European case studies have effectively
traced the way that particular struggles have led to diverse national
gender contracts. In the past seventy years, Sweden has embraced
housewife contracts, equality contracts, equal status contracts, and tran-
sitional contracts at different times (Duncan 1994). Elaborating these
gender regimes not only helps to explain the conundrum of how
"private" forms of patriarchy in industrialized countries came to be
more "public," but also preserves the analytical flexibility to examine
how the gender balance of power may change in the future (Connell
1994).

Most importantly, a feminist approach to the state assumes that
gender is implicated in many facets of any polity. What are the most
important elements we might include in our conception of the gendered
state? At least four aspects need to be examined: the gendered division
of labor within the state apparatus; the gendered structure of power in
the state apparatus; the gendered structure of cathexis (or emotional
attachments); and the interplay between social movements, state policies, and outcomes (Connell 1994; Kofman 1996). As we examine Mexico
with this in mind, it is crucial to note that state actions and state plan-

ning will certainly have an impact on gender relations leading to more or less gender equity in a particular situation.

"Quality" of a Job

In the discussion of Third World industrialization, I suggested that macro-scale analyses were inadequate for measuring the "quality" of development, particularly the "quality" of jobs. One way to assess a job would be to determine the rate of exploitation (or rate of surplus value), given by the ratio of surplus labor to "socially necessary labor time" (surplus labor/socially necessary labor time, or simply s/v). Another way would be to consider what amount of goods and services a particular wage could command. From this, one could determine the adequacy of the wage for a particular standard of living. The worker's lifetime earning would need to be approximated because both productivity and needs vary with age. The skill level of the job and the transferability of skills to other jobs is also an indicator of "quality." Finally, relationships such as the family, wherein one satisfies his or her needs, also must be considered. Like an individual, a family has a beginning, lifetime, and end, so the "family cycle stage" is important in determining the adequacy of the wage (Stichter 1990). We need to know what additional dependent individuals (young and old) must be supported by this wage.

What is missing when a job is assessed by the rate of exploitation or the adequacy of the wage? First of all, there is no way to measure and "subtract" the unhealthy working conditions from the wage. Second, this does not tell us the degree of control a worker has over his or her work situation or the extent to which a worker depends upon the job for sheer survival. Third, certain forms of labor that may be subsidizing the wage within a family, household, or community network are overlooked and undervalued because they are not directly subject to capitalist production relations. These invisible forms of labor include: (1) domestic labor and self-provisioning within the household or family unit and (2) productive labor within the informal sector. A historically contingent gender analysis of the production/reproduction dialectic will complicate the assessment of "quality," but can include these other forms of labor and therefore better explain the quality of work. It thus would be useful to explore the quality of jobs in an area of rapid social transformation such as northern Mexico.

Mexican Industrial Transition

Mexican industry was transformed during the 1980s from state-led import substitution industrialization (ISI) to foreign investment for export production. ISI is a development strategy that uses a variety of techniques (e.g., import licenses, tariffs, subsidized energy inputs) to encourage domestic producers to manufacture goods that have been supplied previously by imports. The transition from ISI to export production was marked by a geographic shift from a centralized industrial core to dispersed northern sites, a change in the nature of the state, and a corresponding reorientation of the state's development strategies. At the same time, a range of policies were reversed to encourage internationalization, liberalization, and privatization of the economy. These transformations did not occur in a vacuum. They influenced and were influenced by the Mexican social structure. Yet there has been no extended examination of gender relations during the transition.[4]

Gender analysis helps to demonstrate how the Mexican state was able to thoroughly transform its state-led production strategy into a neoliberal export-oriented approach. In addition, gender analysis helps explain how and why export production can extract more surplus labor and thus is more successful at attracting international capital. At the same time, the central role of the developmentalist state in the gendering of distinct factory regimes begins to emerge. The state regulated the employment relationship through industrial and social policies that supported distinctly gendered forms of capitalist production. The case studies that follow illustrate that state social programs were unevenly applied and that key aspects were quickly dismantled when the new female-based factory regime in the north supplanted the old male-centered regime in the center.

Before we turn to the gender content of these policies, we might ask, why is industrial policy viewed as the crucial feature of development strategy in the Third World? Industrialization is seen as fundamental because growth in the industrial sector can provide jobs as well as improve technical capacity in the agricultural and service sectors (Kitching 1982). The ISI approach was a creative Latin American solution to the problem of "late" industrialization. After the international economic adjustments associated with the Great Depression and World War II, a comprehensive set of prescriptions was outlined by the United Nations Economic Commission for Latin America (ECLA) to enable Latin American planners to shape their domestic markets while diversifying production. Mexico, Brazil, and Argentina had some success with such programs, as can be seen in their overall growth trajectories. That this single policy was instrumental in Mexico's climb to a semiperipheral status in the global economy is widely accepted. While ISI contributed to a host of problems in Mexico and other Latin American countries, it is important to note that some elements of the ISI strategy survive in the development schemes of contemporary high-growth East Asian countries (that is, the NICs of South Korea, Taiwan, Singapore, and Hong Kong). In these East Asian cases, careful government regulation is the mechanism linking certain elements of ISI to particular aspects of export-oriented production (Evans 1987; Gereffi 1990; Wade 1990a; 1990b).

In Mexico, ISI was the predominant industrial strategy from 1930 until roughly 1976. Nationalistic ideology accompanying this policy made it immensely popular in Mexico and other Latin American countries. The old factory regime connected to Mexican ISI policy also was a concrete manifestation of an intimate alliance between elite state actors and the leaders of organized labor (Middlebrook 1995). The strategy rested on the foundation of a well-paid, stable, and *male* unionized work force. In the mid-1960s, a new factory regime began to emerge on a twenty-kilometer-wide strip of land along the U.S. border. The original enabling legislation–the Border Industrialization Program (or *maquiladora*)–sought to provide employment for seasonal migrant laborers (almost all of whom were male) who had lost their livelihood with the demise of the binational Bracero Program, through which, from 1942 to 1964, Mexican migrants had been officially assigned to agricultural and railroad construction jobs in the United States. The social practices that began as local ad hoc arrangements to replace the Bracero Program quickly matured into a new *national* strategy. An array of new state policies established a new factory regime based on a less organized, lower-paid, female workforce in new cities and regions, undercutting the profitability of the old factory regime. Faced with a changing international political economy, the state began to dismantle the old regime and renegotiate long-standing labor norms in older industrial centers.

Industrial production had been geographically concentrated during the years of the old factory regime (Figure 1.1). Most production took place in Mexico City, Guadalajara and nearby urban sites, with one outlier in the northern city of Monterrey, where early steel production generated a variety of associated manufacturing activities. After industrial transition, the central urban areas around Mexico City (the industrial core) continued to be important industrial sites. However, northern regions (the U.S.-Mexico border area and interior urban sites of

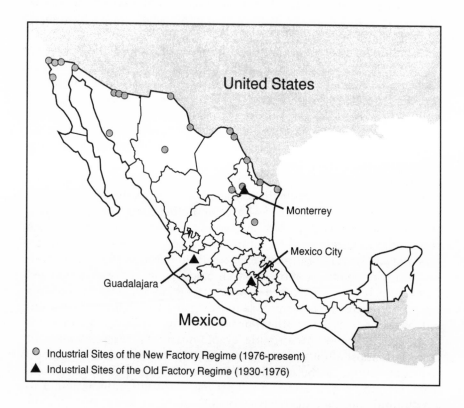

○ Industrial Sites of the New Factory Regime (1976-present)
▲ Industrial Sites of the Old Factory Regime (1930-1976)

Figure 1.1 Two Distinct Factory Regimes

the northern states) attracted more new investment and became the prototype for a new model of accumulation supported and encouraged by a revised state planning strategy. The geographic shift from a central industrial core region to an extensive northern region helped obscure some of the social implications of this profound industrial transition.

The two industrial regions were the result of distinct labor norms, regulatory practices, employers, labor pools, and social policies. The new factory regime has impacted the old factory regime, which in turn has come to resemble the new. I focus on historical and geographic contrasts at their most extreme to explain this rapid and profound transformation in Mexican industrial strategy. Rather than examining particular sectors of industry, which might lend more complexity to the comparison, we medium-sized labor markets and factory regimes shaped by radically dissimilar industrial policies. Nogales, in the state of Sonora, exemplifies the new market-led factory regime. Ciudad Madero in the state of Tamaulipas, represents the previous state-led regime (Figure 1.2). Industry in Nogales is dominated by electronics and other component assembly operations; Ciudad Madero has a long history of petroleum production, as well as small and medium manufacturing enterprises.

The Mexican state used a consistent policy of import substitution industrialization for nearly half a century. What was the social impact of the shift to a market-based strategy? How did industrial restructuring and relocation of industry impact gender and households? Conversely, how did gender relations influence the trajectory of industrial restructuring? What household forms do these industrial workers create and how do the workers organize their own domestic labor? Have changes in federal social programs altered the relationship between workers and the state in the new industrial regions? To begin to answer these questions, we must examine Mexico's maquiladora programs.

The maquiladora program in Mexico was conceived as an imitation of the export oriented growth in the NICs of East Asia. Mexico's Minister of Industry and Commerce, Octaviano Campos Salas, stated clearly to the *Wall Street Journal* (May 25, 1967), "Our idea is to offer free enterprise an alternative to Hong Kong, Japan, and Puerto Rico." From the beginning, Mexico's alternative was based on a young, relatively well-educated, female workforce. A random survey conducted in 1979 of 510 workers in Ciudad Juárez reported that 85 percent were women between the ages of seventeen and twenty-five. Seventy percent were single (Fernández-Kelly 1983b, 214). In recent years the percentage of women in the workforce has fallen to around 70 percent, although the exact proportion of women is difficult to assess from official sources because these data are not disaggregated by job category. Technicians and administrative staff, most of whom are men, are grouped with laborers (Tiano 1990; Staudt 1986). However, overall female employment in the maquiladora was 64.2 percent of the total in 1988 (INEGI, Instituto Nacional de Estadística, Geografía e Informática cited in Sklair 1989, 167).

A number of researchers have explored the implications for household and family formation of the industry's preference for young women (Christopherson 1983a; Fernández-Kelly 1983b, 1987; Young and Christopherson 1986; Staudt 1986; Tiano 1990). Much of this analysis has been done with the results of a survey of 1,236 households in

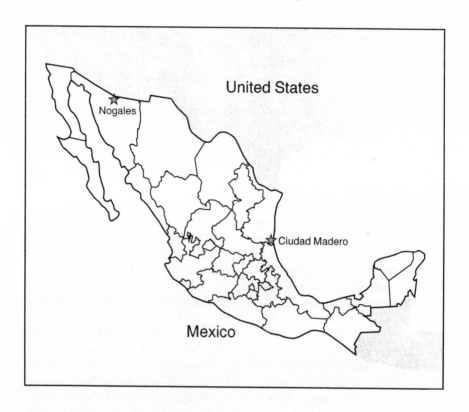

Figure 1.2 Study Sites

Ciudad Juárez, although one study (Tiano's) was done in Mexicali. Maquiladora households tend to be larger, have more female heads-of-household, and to be more female in composition (Christopherson 1983b; Staudt 1986; Tiano 1990). Young and Christopherson (1986) suggest that families of maquiladora workers expand to include extra workers so that there will be a larger income pool in the household. Maquiladora households are more likely to be in debt and have less disposable income, spending more on food and transportation than non-maquiladora households (Christopherson 1983b).

Jobs and family relationships in the maquila industry have little meaning outside their historical context. Unfortunately the historical literature on labor and social reproduction in Mexico is limited and fragmentary. Social historians are only beginning to piece together the changing nature of gender, households, and the family in Mexico. Silvia

Arrom's (1985) penetrating research on the early nineteenth century establishes a foundation for future investigation. She suggests that a powerful ideology of gender roles gave women a morally superior position in the family, but limited their participation in public activities. Women's options and material welfare declined at the same time that these ideas became more popular. There was, however, great variation in this experience by race and by class (Arrom 1985).

Mexican labor history also requires more study. The active role of the state, however, is one of five central themes in this "scarce" literature according to John Womack (1979). Historians agree that a corporatist state has dominated and manipulated labor even in the early mutualist societies that preceded organized labor (Clark 1934; Roxborough 1984).[5] Comparing Mexico to other Latin American states, Guillermo O'Donnell (1978) notes that Mexico's long-standing control of popular and labor groups was unusually stable. This dominance has been institutionalized through state sponsored unions and the broad-based social security agency (IMSS), which encompasses a program of socialized medicine, a daycare tax, and an unemployment/severance fund (Roxborough 1984; Grayson 1989).

The Mexican government began the maquiladora program in 1965 as an aggressive regional promotion of capitalist industrial growth. U.S. manufacturers were invited to move their factories south across the 2,000-mile-long border between the United States and Mexico to take advantage of much lower wage rates. Mexican federal subsidies encouraged the rapid growth of industrial parks, and new regulations allowed manufacturers to import duty-free machinery, parts, and raw materials. The program has been a highly successful accumulation strategy; in its short life span of thirty years, it has been revamped and expanded several times (Schwartz 1987; Sklair 1989).

Through the maquiladora program, Mexico has steadily gained a greater percentage of the export-processing market. In 1987, Mexico produced 12.68 percent of the U.S. imports allowed under Article 806.30 and 807.00 of the Tariff Schedule of the United States, the regulation which is responsible for the global manufacturing phenomenon.[6] Mexico's share of 806/807 production was far ahead of other Third World countries and second only to Japan (Sklair 1989, 12). Mexico remains bound to the NIC export-oriented production model, due to the scope of its international debt, much of it owed to U.S. banks.

The policies of the Mexican government, through executive decrees, have shaped five periods of expansion in the maquiladora program. Oftentimes, informal concessions to specific firms precedes the formal legal changes that have shaped the trajectory of this sector. The first period, between 1965 and 1974, is seen as a time of installation and con-solidation. The geographical scope was expanded during this time and restrictions limiting foreigners to a 49 percent ownership of Mexican firms was relaxed. A recession in the United States threw the industry into a crisis from 1974 to 1976, the second phase of the program. Thousands of workers lost their jobs and many work practices were im-plemented that permitted conditions to fall below the standards of federal labor law. Companies were allowed to adjust the length of the working day at will and probationary periods were lengthened from thirty to ninety days. An expansionary period, from 1976 to 1982, saw several years of 13.8 percent annual growth rate in maquiladora plants (Kopinak 1996). In the years between 1983 and 1989, the most powerful influences on industrial strategy were international pressures for eco-nomic liberalization. Caught in a severe debt crisis, the government re-sponded by trying to turn maquiladoras into permanent industries that could consolidate border development. While considering the evolution of the maquila industry, the important thing to note is that the maquiladora factory regime changed from being the industrial excep-tion to being the rule (Kopinak 1996).

As noted above, the 1970s were critical years for the maquiladora industry. The U.S. recession of 1974 and 1975 produced a sharp downturn in demand for maquiladora products, particularly consumer electronics goods. During the same years, maquiladora workers began militant campaigns for higher wages. Widespread dissatisfaction with the of-ficial unions produced an unsuccessful effort to create a labor movement outside the official unions. There also were numerous plant closures and layoffs during this time.

The percentage of jobs lost was especially high in Nogales, Sonora, the city chosen as a case study of the maquiladora factory regime. After some of the longest and most bitter strikes of the period, the early 1974 maquiladora labor force of 11,000 workers in Nogales had been trimmed to only 5,000 workers by late 1975 (INEGI 1985; Sklair 1989, 104). Employment has climbed since that time and maquiladora employment approached 20,000 by the end of the 1980s (*Arizona Republic* April 18, 1989). Maquiladora jobs are unusually important to the economy of Nogales. Among border cities as a whole, 10.4 percent of the economi-cally active worked in maquiladoras in 1980. In Nogales, this propor-tion was 49.5 percent, higher than any other maquiladora city (Perlo Cohen 1987, 160).

Nogales is unique among Mexican maquiladora towns in having a number of dormitories for maquiladora workers in which workers are crowded into unhealthy living conditions (Denman 1991; Feagin 1991).

Dormitory housing is also widespread in other export processing zones in Malaysia, Thailand, Taiwan, and South Korea (Fuentes and Ehrenreich 1983; Grossman 1979; Bello and Rosenfeld 1990). By contrast, worker dormitories are not common in Mexico and have not been discussed in the popular or academic literature. Although the use of worker dormitories in Asia has been noted, no detailed studies exist of social reproduction within the dormitories.

The dormitories are primarily of interest because the workers are still under control beyond the shop floor and after working hours. The factory regime penetrates into the daily lives of these workers. However, there are a number of other reasons to examine these dormitories. First, the buildings themselves physically separate the workers from the rest of the community. Second, family relations are at least temporarily broken when a family member takes a job and chooses dormitory housing. A large dormitory household becomes a new "family," in which many of the workers' daily reproductive needs are now met. Third, since the job is a prerequisite for the housing, the arrangement is insecure. Sickness, pregnancy, even personality conflict, can result in both job and housing loss. Fourth, it is interesting that in Mexico dormitories are being used only in Nogales, whereas they are common throughout export processing zones in Asia.

Throughout the book I will be elaborating on the descriptions of two distinct factory regimes, which I refer to as the old factory regime and the new factory regime (Figure 1.1 and Table 1.2). The data for this comparison are drawn from two urban case studies: Ciudad Madero provides a case study of the old and Nogales is a case study of the new. Although I refer to these as the old and the new factory regimes, I must emphasize that I am contrasting two comprehensive regimes of production and *reproduction*. A total social system of state-led production/reproduction was superseded by a total social system of market-led production/reproduction. The old regime was an integral part of Mexico's import substitution national development strategy for four-and-one-half decades. The new regime contribute to an overarching transnational, export-oriented system that has become a new national model of development.

The central objective of my research is to explore the changing relationship between the state and the household in a Third World factory regime. As I have indicated, we already have ample evidence that the introduction of export-processing industries has reshaped the household and the family, both in Mexico and throughout the Third World. Households adopt a variety of makeshift survival strategies: they change their composition, change their marriage and childbirth pat-

Table 1.2 Main Aspects of the Two Factory Regimes

	Old Factory Regime (1930-1978)	New Factory Regime (1976-present)
Location	Centralized (Mexico City and nearby)	Northern region, dispersed sites
Strategy	•State-led ISI •Domestic market orientation •Some Fordist aspects (effort to increase production)	•Market-led neoliberal •Export orientation •Some Post-Fordist aspects (effort to lower cost of social reproduction)
Production practices	•Family wage (male); high •Fully proletarianized •State-owned enterprises •State support for unions •Workforce unionized •Regulation of the labor-capital relation •Subsidy to domestic capital	•Individual wage (female and male); low •Some small miscellaneous nonwage income sources •TNCs are predominant •Unions under attack •Workforce less organized •Deregulation of the labor-capital relation •Subsidy to transnational capital
Reproduction practices	•Nuclear household •Domestic labor done by housewife •State social programs •Public child care •Worker housing assistance •Public medical care for worker and family	•Various household forms •Intense negotiation of domestic labor; some male labor •Social goods bound tightly to employment relationship •Private (household) child care •Severe housing shortage, many acquire outside the market •Health care is commodified, some doctors within factories •State retrenchment; programs underfunded in northern region; social provision by larger TNCs

terns, or find supplementary informal sources of income. These and other strategies are clearly contingent on particular local and regional situations. It also is clear from the literature that the state exerts a strong influence on these contingencies through the means it uses to facilitate industrialization, as well as by defining the nature and extent of social provision. Burawoy's work (1985) suggests that states are providing less worker protection and fewer social benefits. Very little is known about this process in the Third World. My research contributes to the literature by exploring the pattern of state retrenchment and its effect on three groups of workers: (1) Ciudad Madero workers of public and private industries; (2) residents of squatter households in Nogales; and (3) residents of single-sex dormitories in Nogales.

The first group represents an earlier model of industrial development, the state-led factory regime. These are state-employed petroleum workers and private industry workers in Ciudad Madero. Many of them live in state supplied housing provided through a state-run workers housing program, Instituto Nacional del Fondo de la Vivienda para los Trabajadores (INFONAVIT). Although all employers in Mexico must pay the equivalent of 5 percent of their monthly wage totals into the fund (more than three million houses were built with this money between 1972 and 1982) maquiladora owners have complained that they see little state housing in the border cities (Grayson 1989, 54; *Twin Plant News*, May 1990).

The second group consists of maquiladora workers living with their families in squatter settlements on hillsides in Nogales. This group is representative of the vast majority of maquiladora workers and therefore prefigures a new model of development in Mexico. The third group represents one of several variations in this evolving model. These workers live in eight former factory buildings that maquiladora owners have converted into residential dormitories. The owners regulate and administer the housing. The dormitory system is both a highly flexible and a highly profitable enterprise. With minimal difficulty, the labor pool can be increased or decreased on a weekly basis in order to meet the needs of twenty different subcontractor assembly operations. The entire day is regimented for workers who live in the dorm and pay a weekly fee for an individual bunk bed and locker.

The research probes the origins of the new factory regime in the context of Nogales, Sonora, and the emergence of a household form that (for industrial workers) is unique to this locality. These are the single-sex worker dormitories operated by transnational corporations–a household form in which social reproduction becomes an extension of the labor process itself. The corporations clearly helped to establish the dormitories, but were any public officials at the local, state, or federal level involved? Was there any resistance to their creation? Why were these dormitories, which have been prominent in East Asian industrialization, been established in only one city with maquiladoras?

Three theses guide the research. First, the maquiladora program represents a decrease in the "quality" of employment in Mexico, in part through decreased levels of state provision of social benefits (i.e., housing, health care, employment security, piped water, and electricity). Second, households and families reorganize and find ways to compensate for some of the cuts; they also must turn to the market for some of the previously provided goods. Third, welfare cuts were relatively more onerous for dormitory residents because the dormitory arrangement was the result of increased worker vulnerability during the U.S. recession of the mid-1970s which took an extreme form in Nogales. More control is exerted over the lives of dormitory residents through specification and control of activities after working hours. Furthermore, the dormitory arrangement reduces industry's cost of workforce reproduction, because only the individual is being sustained, rather than an entire family.

Notes

1. Social reproduction is defined as the tasks involved in the daily and generational restoration of workers, encompassing mundane household chores (i.e., laundry, meal preparation, cleaning) as well as child care and biological reproduction. It includes work that is not directly part of the wage labor system but yet is essential to the long-term maintenance of this system. Using this definition, recent feminist scholarship continues to unearth forgotten realms of work, such as domestic work, the production of children, and emotional work, which had not been previously theorized.

2. The concept of factory regime is borrowed from Michael Burawoy (1985) and encompasses the apparatus of production regulation (i.e., labor and business law, labor and business bureaucracy, grievance boards) and the organization of the labor process.

3. Neoliberal policies are based on the liberalization of the economy toward a "free market" ideal. State intervention in most economic activities is seen as an anathema to those who would advocate neoliberal projects.

4. The work of Lourdes Benería (1992) details the effects of structural adjustment on Mexican households. See also her innovative theorizing of gender and class connections and her research on Mexican households that participate in subcontracting arrangements with industrial producers in Mexico City (Benería and Sen 1982; Benería and Roldán 1987).

5. These early forms of labor organization were little more than sick and death benefit associations. Railway workers were instrumental in two early efforts: the Supreme Order of Mexican Railway employees, formed in 1888, and the Confederation of Railway Societies of the Mexican Republic, established in 1897.

The latter organization had an influence on the development of contemporary railway unions (Clark 1934).

6. 806/807 significantly reduced the costs to transnational corporations of manufacturing outside the United States by charging duty only on the value added (usually labor cost) of goods assembled elsewhere. Machinery, vehicles, parts, and anything else needed for processing are imported into Mexico duty free for transformation, assembly, or other processing.

2

Early Industrialization in Mexico

> It was considered to be in the interest of the state, as well as of the landed class, that both the industrial and the agricultural workers should be kept ignorant, servile, unorganized, and un-class conscious. It did not, seemingly, occur to the government that protection of the worker was either necessary or desirable. A cheap labor supply was one of the principal inducements held forth to foreign capitalists. (Marjorie Clark 1934. *Organized Labor in Mexico*, p. 4.)

Gender and *social reproduction* are invisible in most narratives of Mexican economic and industrial development. These two concepts are useful tools to apply to an examination of the three phases of industrial growth in Mexico, and will yield a deeper understanding of the transitions between the phases. Because this research is focused on the social pressures that caused the second phase to dissolve into the third, the discussion is more carefully elaborated for the transition in the mid-1970s, when the state dismantled a national arrangement that had extended social welfare benefits to industrial workers and their families (Table 2.1).

The first two periods of industrial growth could be seen as state-led, although the consequences for workers were quite different. In the first period the state's priority was to maintain order so that capitalist expansion could proceed. This entailed the forced proletarianization of the peasantry in many regions and the repression of labor movements. During the second period, the state also pursued a capitalist project while regulating the employment relationship and pursuing direct production. Gender relations have been reshaped by these early factory

Table 2.1. Three Periods of Mexican Industrialization

	Porfian state-led	Revolutionary state-led	Market-led
	1890-1930	1930-1976	1976-present
Women:	peasant production	housewifization	female proletarianization
Social reproduction:	peasant extended family	state provision and nuclear family	individualization with increasing nucleation and resistance
Workers:	proletarianization and repression	nuclear family with male wage	individualization
Triple alliance:	state dominant	state dominant	foreign capital dominant

regimes. These gender consequences are somewhat obscure in the historical data on industrialization, but begin to emerge if we examine the changing dynamics of social reproduction. As we turn to the case studies in Chapters three, four, and five, these gender consequences will become more apparent.

The First Wave of Industrialization, 1890 to 1930

Several thousand manufacturing plants as well as mining, transportation (i.e., railroad building), and oil production operations flourished in Mexico in the late nineteenth century. Workers, predominantly males, were drawn into industrial employment as they were violently forced from their land or squeezed by debt peonage. Peasant production on large semi-feudal properties known as haciendas, was the only alternative for most of these men. The new industrial jobs were not typically considered permanent, nor were wages considered to be family wages, so most women who partnered with these men remained in extended social networks that characterized pre-capitalist agricultural production. That is, although we have few detailed accounts of their lives, many of the women who were involved with industrial workers in this period were involved in peasant productive and social reproductive work.

Many of the social reproductive activities of industrial workers of the period thus were outside of the industrial capitalist realm. Circulating between temporary industrial jobs and peasant networks, male workers were subsidized by extended family networks that could provide some of their basic needs. Thus, due to interlocking peasant networks of mutual support, wages of industrial workers were not the sole means of support for the worker or his family. This was somewhat less true for those rural workers who lived on those haciendas which operated as capitalist enterprises. Rather than paying rent with a portion of the season's yield as had been done in the past, these workers often were required to participate in wage labor in mining or commercial operations in order to meet their rent.

Given these labor conditions, how did Mexico achieve industrial growth at the close of the nineteenth century? In a remarkably short time, dictator Porfirio Díaz and his government created entire industrial sectors by authorizing and subsidizing monopoly enterprises. A concerted industrial policy directed by an authoritarian state helped to produce an industrial capitalist class and a diversified material base including steel, textiles, glass, and minerals. The program was intertwined with two larger projects that were already in motion by 1890: the centralization of political authority and a single-minded strategy of capitalist accumulation based on foreign investment and the export of primary products. The incipient factory regime must be seen within the context of this sustained agro-export boom that was the result of cooperation between regional *caciques* and Díaz. In the 1880s, Díaz began to encourage foreign direct investment, particularly within the mining, agricultural, transportation (i.e., railroad-building) and oil sectors. This influx of foreign capital fostered an export boom that enabled the dictator and his *científicos* to further consolidate power and undertake a series of structural reforms.[1]

Diaz's systematic transformation of property relationships altered the hacienda system and resulted in debt peonage, a condition that resembled slavery, for many rural producers, whether male or female. This exacerbated the inequities that already characterized most rural areas, where the vast Mexican peasantry produced a surplus for a tiny landlord class. An 1883 land law allowed foreign land companies to acquire one-fifth of the total land mass of Mexico in only eleven years. Direct seizure of private and communal lands also was common.

A new group of domestic capitalists was nurtured by industrial promotion programs during these years. Many of these early capitalists were European-born merchant-financiers who knew very little about industry and whose enterprises remain among Mexico's present-day industrial giants (Haber 1989, 67). Foreign capital was important to manufacturing as well, although it was concentrated in the sectors of railroad construction, mining, and petroleum and contributed only twenty-nine percent of overall manufacturing capital (King 1970, 5). How then did Díaz persuade domestic merchant-financial capitalists to assume the risks of industrial investment?

Díaz and his advisers devised a set of complementary policies to cajole this group into manufacturing activities, granting federal concessions, maintaining a system of strict control over labor, and restructuring the tariff system. New industrialists were able to maximize profits by keeping prices high and wages low. By contrast, importers of manufactured goods saw their profits fall when duties on their goods were raised markedly in the late 1880s and foreign tariff schedules were again revised upward in 1892, 1893, 1896, and 1906. Internal tariffs (subnational state and municipal), a principal source of revenue for some states, were abolished in 1896. The domestic industrialists, therefore, enjoyed uniform access to markets within Mexico and uniform protection beyond. Federal concessions initially granted tax-exempt status to larger manufacturing enterprises for a period of seven and thirty years. By 1893, a blanket exemption from direct federal taxes and customs duties on the machinery and other building material was extended to all new industries capitalized in excess of 250,000 pesos. The required minimum capitalization was lowered to 100,000 pesos five years later.

Some of the early industrial enterprises processed goods that were linked to the booming market in agriculture and minerals. And the growth of a waged workforce in the primary sector helped to increase demand for manufactured goods. During this "first wave of industrialization . . . the production of a wide range of staples, including steel, cement, beer, cotton textiles, paper, glass, dynamite, soap and cigarettes, came to be dominated by large vertically integrated firms that utilized mass production techniques to satisfy the mass market" (Haber 1989, 3).[2]

Most factories continued production during the years of the Mexican Revolution, 1910 to 1920, and were physically undamaged by the fighting. Likewise, many of the monopolies and oligopolies that relied on government protection survived virtually unscathed (Womack 1978, 84; Haber 1989, 124).[3] Industrial capitalists quickly aligned themselves with military commanders and political leaders concerned with rebuilding the government apparatus. In November 1917, a national conference of industrialists was convened in Mexico City. Regional associations of industrialists underscored the importance of tariff protection to the new government and expressed their opposition to the new Constitution's labor protections (Haber 1989, 139).

The impact of the Revolution on the landlord class is far less clear. Many standard historical interpretations suggested that the *hacendados* were eliminated. In fact, this was only the case in a few districts (Womack 1978, 98). Land ownership remained highly concentrated even in 1940, when two-fifths of the country's farm and ranch land was held in very large estates of 10,000 hectares or more (Womack 1978). It is important to point out that many estates were not technically haciendas but functioned as capitalist firms before the Revolution. Others may have maintained pre-capitalist agricultural production, while diversifying into mining and other commercial activities. It is clear that many wealthy landholders maintained their wealth during the Revolution and continued in some mix of capitalist and pre-capitalist production after it.

There also was a considerable measure of continuity for many large foreign enterprises, which operated in Mexico during the Revolutionary years. And throughout the 1920s, U.S. assets increased in relation to British investments. Only during the Depression did aggregate foreign ownership decline briefly.[4] Although many employers continued to operate in Mexico, the militancy of the workers changed during this period, as well as the conditions of work and the willingness of the state to regulate the workplace. In short, a new factory regime began to emerge toward the end of the Revolution. This factory regime was consolidated with new labor laws and in the reactions to the external shock of the Great Depression.

Despite the persistence of hacendados and foreign enterprises, the structure of authority was clearly disrupted during the Revolutionary years. In the early 1920s, immediately afterward, central power was especially weak, since it was maintained through personal ties between former military commanders. A struggle for power among these leaders and various regional alliances was contained by the ascendance of the "Sonoran dynasty" in mid-decade and the formation of a national political party and independent party bureaucracy.[5] During these early years of state-building, the reconstruction of the financial system and the negotiation of the external debt formed the basis for the conservative policy inclination within the government (Maxfield 1990).

The legacy of these early years of industrial promotion bore fruit in the nearly unrivaled pace of growth after 1940. The large enterprises that had been nurtured by the Porfirian state had been built and operated with capital-intensive imported machinery. The census reported fifty-five hundred manufacturing industries in 1902. When conditions again became favorable for capital accumulation, the considerable excess capacity of these plants was already in place.

State-Led Industrialization, 1930 to 1976

The second major period of industrial expansion had consequences for gender relations among industrial workers. Formal sector workers, who were still predominantly male, were directly incorporated into the state apparatus through industrial promotion schemes. Thus the social pact between labor and the state that characterized the period could also be seen as a national gender contract, because it institutionalized the personal relationships between men and women who were drawn into high-growth sectors of the economy. Industrial policies and social policies which presumed a universal male worker, in fact re-inscribed, reinforced, and reworked existing gender hierarchies in the comprehensive factory regime that emerged during these years. In a quasi-Fordist arrangement, a nuclear family ideal was encouraged through a male wage package that was conceived as a family wage. By contrast, women were written into social and economic policy as mothers and housewives.

Since this post-Revolutionary era of the early 1920s, workers' collective projects have evolved in close collaboration with the modern Mexican state. Parallel projects of consolidating a nation-state and cultivating a network of labor unionists helped to produce identical geographical patterns during the years of import substitution industrialization (ISI): a centralized and concentrated network of production sites and a centralized regulatory apparatus to oversee labor relations at these sites. As we have seen, geographical patterns of production during the ISI years were striking. With the exception of steel and related industries that had been located near the source of extensive iron ore deposits in Monterrey, industrial production was concentrated in the central urban areas, particularly in Mexico City. Guadalajara, to the west of the capital, was a secondary industrial location. The state's regulatory apparatus displayed an analogous pattern. Power was highly concentrated in a hierarchical set of institutions clustered in Mexico City. The structure of the labor unions themselves and their network of national federations also took on a hierarchical form in which power was highly concentrated in central Mexico. The emergence of these patterns underscores the extent to which the two processes were interconnected during these years.

The close connection between political consolidation and collective labor organizing did not result in co-optation of the popular class-based, male-dominated labor movement. On the contrary, the two projects were highly interdependent. The state-building impulse gave strength to the labor movement and vice versa. The relationship also had a cyclical character, in which periods of increased state control alternated with cycles of greater labor militancy. At times, however, labor militancy was explicitly encouraged by the state, and, throughout the period, labor unions–through their intimate alliance with the federal state and through its regulatory framework–enjoyed a superior position in the labor/capital relation. Nonunion workers did not receive these special privileges, however, and in many respects subsidized the protected position of industrial workers.

Political elites, in order to retain their power, used two strategies to institutionalize worker participation in the emerging polity. Within the larger project of state-building, they first developed a comprehensive regulatory framework that established specialized agencies to mediate labor conflicts and provide social services to workers, as we will see below. In addition to this regulatory apparatus, the new national leadership employed a second strategy, creating a political alliance with the emerging industrial labor movement.

Thus the reorganization of social reproduction was a fundamental part of the social pact between government-business-labor that characterized this period. The state became directly involved in social reproductive activities by rapidly expanding public social budgets and providing a range of social programs. Education, health, housing, and child care were all socialized to some extent during these years. Students throughout the country were provided with free textbooks and a free education because popular literacy was deemed essential for good citizenship. While social benefits were unevenly distributed, the overarching goal of these years was to progressively increase social funds in order to improve social equity. Toward this end, social programs were designed and implemented at the federal level. The allocation of a substantial portion of federal revenues to the social budget demonstrates a major public commitment to social reproductive activities. Of course, many social reproductive activities continued to be privately performed within households, but even these "private" activities were reshaped by comprehensive education, health, housing, and child care programs. The impact of the social program was especially pronounced for those households that had been drawn into the privileged industrial sectors of the economy. These effects become more evident when we begin to examine, decade-by-decade, the evolution of the state-led factory regime.

The 1931 federal labor code provided a foundation for a new institutional arrangement among government-labor-business actors (Roxborough 1984; Middlebrook 1991). Based on social justice criteria set forth in the Constitution, conciliation and arbitration boards adjudicated labor disputes in a federal system with subsidiary regional branches. The subsequent ambitious effort to industrialize and restructure Mexico's economy was at first assembled in a piecemeal fashion, as state and society struggled to survive the twin insults of the Mexican Revolution and the Great Depression.

Post-revolutionary class structure was relatively unchanged in spite of the fact of widespread mobilization. An uneasy alliance between the emerging urban working class and the peasantry did not survive the war. Distance between these two groups further increased as they were brought into distinct bureaucratic arms of the government. The reoganization of the govenment's sectorial organizations divided urban from rural workers (i.e., peasants and agricultural workers were removed to a separate sector).[6] A public focus on rural reform (and away from manufacturing) during the 1930s further inoculated these two groups against a collective agenda. The agrarian project involved the distribution of land to small producers.

The Mexican Regional Labor Confederation (CROM) coordinated the urban-based labor movement but its various rival factions were replaced in 1936 by the hierarchical and cohesive Confederation of Mexican Workers (CTM) as one sector of the governing party. Both groups were comprised of predominantly male workers represented by exclusively male leadership. The sectorial structure of government reinforced the national political position of organized labor, with labor as one of four powerful branches. Having experienced their collective power during the Revolutionary years, popular forces demanded explicit government support for unions and labor rights–which in turn ignited further labor mobilizations. The strength of labor culminated in the dramatic and highly symbolic expropriation and nationalization of foreign petroleum enterprises in 1938. Thereafter, petroleum workers worked directly for the state and lobbied successfully for collective influence on workplace organization and for generous wage and benefit packages. Their success set an independent example of labor-friendly workplace norms for capitalist employers. Public sector industrial employment would be expanded rapidly in the years to come. In addition to these effects, the expropriation of foreign petroleum enterprises late in the decade also was an immensely popular act that legitimated the centralization of public power in the state because it was framed in nationalist rhetoric.

Although the landlord class survived the Revolution, the popular mobilization had earned the new state a certain measure of autonomy from hacendados and capitalists alike. Due to the sudden contraction of export revenue during the Great Depression, the state also secured slightly more room to experiment with economic policies. The state's authority was unchallenged because it was clear to capitalists and other property holders that Mexico's problems required radical measures. In 1932, Mexico moved to end convertibility of the exchange rate and began to pursue expansionist monetary and fiscal policies. This raised the cost of imports. In addition, the drastic deterioration in the external terms of trade in the early 1930s stimulated a transfer of resources into production for the domestic market and a spontaneous substitution of consumer durables (Kaufman 1990). Thus, while struggling to avoid a balance of payments crisis, state bureaucrats embraced a set of reactive policies that later would become the foundation of the ISI program.

Combined with the incorporation of popular forces into the state apparatus, these actions changed the relationship between the state and capital. Domestic capitalists were uneasy with some government actions in the 1930s. The bankers' alliance (i.e., private bankers, large-scale traders, industrialists, and public sector monetary authorities) supported policies that promoted private capital accumulation, yet struggled with the populist Cárdenas coalition over the means to pursue this goal. In addition, capitalists resisted the incorporation of popular sectors in the ruling party. Of course, international capitalists were even more outspoken about their displeasure, complaining bitterly over the oil property nationalizations. Although the companies involved were well compensated, foreign capitalists feared that such nationalist acts foreshadowed the destruction of other avenues for private capital accumulation. The state, however, did not at first interfere with most operations of international capital.

The state-led factory regime that was characteristic of the 1930 to 1976 period coalesced into a fairly stable arrangement in the 1940s. Some of the most important features of the social pact with labor, such as the regulation of workplaces and the broad public commitment to worker social programs, were consolidated during this decade. The gendering of the industrial development model also became clear during this decade, as female citizens continued to be represented, constrained, and encouraged in their roles as mothers and housewives in numerous social and economic policies. The most significant social program, in terms of the amount of resources and the number of people served, was the establishment of the Instituto Mexicano de Seguro Social (IMSS) which began providing free health care and social services to workers and their families in 1943. Created with a loan of 500 million pesos from the Finance Ministry it was subsequently funded by contributions from employers, employees, and the state. The social security law that created IMSS in 1939 also established a variety of worker protections against accidents, disability, sickness, and unemployment. [7]

A crucial turning point in Mexico's economic policy was the way in which Avila Camacho's regime (1940 to 1946) began to reverse the nationalist-populist mobilizations of the 1930s. Land reform was curtailed in favor of the promotion of capitalist agribusiness techniques. International prices for fibers and edible oils rose during World War II and these revenues provided a subsidy to ISI strategy while legitimating an increased public investment in agribusiness, through such things as massive investments in irrigation infrastructure. These policies, coupled with the reduced pace of popular mobilization, soothed the concerns of the capitalist class. Their antagonism gave way to a broad business-state alliance in the 1940s that supported industrialization. World War II helped to cement this alliance by providing a rationale for further public intervention in the economy. This alliance between capitalists and the state deepened as the policies of the war years created a "new group" of industrial capitalists, distinct from the financial-industrial conglomerates of the past (Mosk 1950).

Critical to understanding this period is the coalescence of financiers and industrialists into powerful conglomerate *grupos* that prospered during the state-led development effort (Maxfield 1990). The close linkage of financial and industrial capital that had been evident since the turn of the century and that persisted throughout the Revolutionary period made these *grupos* almost immune to state efforts to guide industrial development. In fact, some of the elements of national planning were defeated, manipulated, or quickly rescinded under pressure from business groups. Industrial groups themselves were reconfigured during the war years. Within the corporatist political structure, business groups were aligned in Camaras Nacionales de Comercio y Industrias (CONACOMIN), the National Chambers of Trade and Industry which Camacho divided into separate commercial and industrial chambers in 1941. Within the industrial chamber a semi-autonomous chamber was created for manufacturing enterprises (CANICINTRA). This group was "the indirect product of the state's industrialization programs" (Maxfield 1990, 48). The industry group that formed in 1929 in opposition to the new government's labor laws, Coparmex, remained independent of the corporatist structure.

While many aspects of the new factory regime took shape during the 1940s, it must be emphasized that these policies were far more experimental than is often recognized. Early policies were geared to short-term goals, without much consideration of the long-term effects (Kaufman 1990). As the policies accumulated, however, the overall package was enormously successful at industrial promotion and growth. There were protectionist elements in the overall strategy, but government promotion (of industry) was more significant. Industrial policy was implemented through banking and other legal changes.

Nacional Financiera, (Nafinsa)[8] was restructured in 1940 and assumed a critical role in the financing of industrial promotion. As one of several development banks created in 1934, Nafinsa shaped Mexico's import-substitution strategy by funding and creating new industries, specifically compensating for those manufactured goods that became unavailable during the war. Nafinsa acquired great amounts of capital to support new industries through increased reserve requirement on private banks. A key strategy in the Nafinsa effort was to create industries that could provide low-cost intermediate inputs to other industries, e.g., steelmaking, fertilizers, railroad cars, diesel trucks, and cement. The "new industrialists" of these sectors did not have sufficient capital to begin these operations and the older *grupos* were reluctant to risk their assets in potentially less-profitable endeavors. In fact, the oligopolies consistently resisted the new industries that Nafinsa created. Toward the end of the war, the creation of state-owned firms became a priority. Strategic sectors, such as communication and transportation, electrical generation, energy, and mining became the targets of state investment and control, as well as industries that could provide low-cost inputs to other manufacturers (Cypher 1990).

The passage of the *Ley de Industrias de Transformación*, the Manufacturing Industries Law, proved to be a turning point in industrial policy. It exempted "new" and "necessary" industries from a wide range of taxes, import licensing fees, and quotas in 1941 (Cypher 1990, 53). Necessary firms were defined as those national manufacturers that were needed to satisfy existing internal demand. A 1945 law extended the federal tax exemption for up to ten years. Designed to protect wartime industries from competition, the law also benefited many of the largest manufacturing firms that were not Nafinsa owned and financed. A sharp rise in tariffs in 1941 provided some protection for domestic industries. A new comprehensive system of import licensing introduced in 1944 was even more effective. Through import licenses, policymakers had near absolute control over the quantity of imports. During World War II, the state made an effort to limit foreign direct investment. An emergency decree required foreign investors to get federal permission to invest. A number of strategic industries were closed to foreign companies. Through this policy of "Mexicanization," the state showed a preference for companies with majority Mexican ownership but the practice was loosely enforced on a case-by-case basis until the 1960s when it was more strictly enforced (Story 1986; Cypher 1990).

Restrictions on labor autonomy were particularly evident in the 1940s, as the Mexican economy began to expand at such a rate that it was widely invoked as a development "miracle." Radical groups (especially those based in powerful national industrial unions) mobilized to such an extent that the state/labor alliance was threatened. Seeking a measure of autonomy from the state, radicals formed a rival labor confederation in 1947. In response, the government purged the member organizations (railroad, petroleum, mining-metalworking, and telephone workers) of their independent leaders and by the early 1950s had defeated the "most important labor opposition movement in Mexican history" (Middlebrook 1991; de la Garza 1993). The radical leaders were replaced with hand-picked leaders who were willing to behave in a more cooperative manner. Government-imposed union leaders have since been known by the deprecatory term "cowboys" (*Charros*), from the nickname of one of these leaders.[9] This defeat of an independent labor union movement in the late 1940s consolidated the CTM/PRI alliance in a very resilient form that remained basically unchanged for nearly four decades (Middlebrook 1995).

The period from 1958 to 1970 is commonly referred to as the time of "stabilized growth" in which a model of industrial growth based on foreign borrowing became more explicitly articulated. Proponents of this approach argued that the only constraint on growth was the lack of domestic savings. They suggested that returns on industrial investment would finance the cost of international loans for the purchase of machinery and equipment. Industrialists were encouraged to finance capital-intensive factories with foreign loans and to import machinery, which was exempt from the high tariffs applied to other imports. The earlier policy of Mexicanization (i.e., the requirement of a 51 percent minimum Mexican ownership) was strongly enforced during these years through the selective denial of import licenses and tax exemptions to companies that did not have majority Mexican ownership. In other efforts to limit the operation of foreign capital in strategic industries, electric power companies were nationalized in 1960, foreign mining operations were proscribed in 1961, and Mexicanization of the rapidly expanding auto parts manufacture was strictly enforced.

Some problems with the state-led development model were already evident during this period of growth, while others only gradually became more apparent. Capital flight was a persistent concern, one with which successive administrations have had to grapple. Much like the issue of a highly regressive tax structure that was the subject of renewed struggle in 1964 because it taxed the poor at a higher rate, the state repeatedly proved unable to impose discipline on the capitalist class. Another difficulty was the lack of adequate investment in technical aspects of higher education, especially for research and development activities that could enhance industrial potential (Cypher 1990). Growth rates slowed in the mid-1960s as economic stagnation set in. Furthermore, Mexico's budget deficit more than doubled in the five years from 1965 to 1970, soaring from $367 million to $946 million (Teichman 1988, 39). This deficit in the current account led to an increased reliance on foreign borrowing that would eventually undo the Mexican "miracle" of sustained high growth rates.

Some of the difficulties of the late 1960s were inherent in the ISI model of development. For example, industrial promotion eclipsed the needs of the agricultural sector (Barkin 1990). Neglect gradually stifled agricultural output, particularly among small producers using marginal unimproved lands. From the mid-1960s onward, agricultural growth fell below the population growth rate (Fitzgerald 1985, 216). This led to an increase in the demand for food imports in the 1960s and to spiraling food prices. Ironically, this chain of consequences also defeated the purpose of ISI to some extent (Barkin 1990).

During these years, government actors were involved in the second and most difficult stage of implementation. Having been successful at the substitution of consumer goods products, economic planners began an assault on intermediate and capital goods markets.[10] Mexico accelerated foreign borrowing and began to expand commodity exports and manufactured exports in order to acquire enough foreign exchange to finance the imports necessary for secondary ISI (Gereffi 1990, 21). In addition, foreign investment was encouraged in intermediate and capital goods industries while Mexican public investment was increasingly channeled to transportation and industry (Cockcroft 1983, 179; Teichman 1988, 37).

Over and above these structural economic problems, the state-led model was also beginning to generate political costs. A neglect of the agricultural sector fueled high levels of unemployment and underemployment in the late 1960s, reaching a combined total of 40 to 50 percent by official estimate (Tello cited in Teichman 1988, 39). Moreover, the state-led factory regime exacerbated income inequalities so that the distribution of income was among the most skewed in contemporary global experience.[11] Those who were excluded from the benefits of the social pact with labor became increasingly vocal. Unions agitated for better wages, while peasants and urban residents stepped up the pace of invading land for settlement. Popular unrest was met by increased state repression, culminating in the tragic 1968 Tlatelolco massacre in Mexico City.[12]

The second period of Mexican state-led development strategy was first implemented during an international depression and took shape during the subsequent economic disruptions of World War II. However, the Mexican model matured and prospered during the unprecedented and more lengthy period of international capital expansion that followed World War II. Global production levels soared during these years, while global financial markets exploded in both volume and extent. Worldwide financial flows grew to exceed the flow of goods by a factor of fifty to one (Spero 1990, 50). Since the explosion of finance capital intensified the need to recycle capital into profitable activities, Mexico and other developing countries provided an outlet for excess capital liquidity in the international banking system.

The internationalization of finance capital was accompanied by a process of labor market internationalization which began to create a "new international division of labor" (NIDL) in the late 1960s. In the outmoded division of labor, Third World countries like Mexico had been the producers of primary products: minerals and agricultural commodities. With the NIDL, labor intensive industrial tasks tend to be transferred to peripheral, low-wage countries, while highly skilled industrial tasks remain in the high-wage countries of the core (Froebel, Heinrichs and Kreye 1980).

The transition to a NIDL has been explained by technological improvements and by the changing global conditions of the valorization and accumulation of capital. Productive capital increased its mobility in response to a profit squeeze in the advanced capitalist countries. Low unemployment and increased trade union activity in the period of growth following World War II strengthened the working class in advanced capitalist countries so that profit rates began to fall in the late 1960s and industrial capitalists began to relocate their operations to the Third World. The fragmentation of the production process into operations that could be performed by semi-skilled workers also facilitated the NIDL (Froebel, Heinrichs, and Kreye 1980; Corbridge 1986; Peet 1987; Jenkins 1988).

Increased capital flows, both productive capital associated with NIDL and unregulated speculative capital, had caused severe strains in the Bretton Woods system by the late 1960s.[13] The internationalization of production, the internationalization of banking, and the growth of the Eurocurrency market were several new forms of monetary independence that produced crises in exchange rates and interfered with national economic management (Thrift 1988; Spero 1990; Corbridge 1993). As U.S. economic hegemony eroded in the late 1960s, the strains led to a paralysis in the global regulatory system during the late 1960s and early 1970s.

International issues had a great influence on Mexico's development trajectory during the 1970s. The Bretton Woods financial system was finally abrogated when U.S. president Richard Nixon abandoned the gold standard. Although the same major institutions continued to manage the international financial system, they have struggled to restore order to the international system. A variety of attempts at powerful alliances (i.e., meetings of the Group of Seven and Group of Ten, establishment of the European Monetary System) have endeavored to construct a monetary system or systems that would be managed multilaterally. These efforts have been successful at avoiding some acute international problems but no definitive management system has emerged to replace Bretton Woods. In the interim, fixed exchange rates have been abandoned resulting in highly unstable exchange rates between major world currencies. The U.S. dollar remains an important reserve asset, but the Mark, the Yen, as well as Special Drawing Rights[14] (SDRs) have become significant rivals, especially during the 1980s when U.S. balance of payments weakened.

The unprecedented rate of global economic expansion in the years after World War II contributed to Mexico's state-led growth strategy by facilitating large capital flows from foreign sources into Mexico. In the early 1970s, the increased volume of these flows to Mexico (and other Third World countries) occurred at the precise moment when the rules of international finance were being reformulated, and bound Mexico ever more tightly to the international financial community. The contradictions of this increasing expansion to vulnerable developing economies precipitated a profound debt crisis in Mexico (and elsewhere) in the 1980s. In turn, the fiscal crisis in Mexico reduced the state's capacity to shape policy because constraints were imposed by international lenders. Through the same process, the position and influence of foreign capital in Mexico were strengthened.

In examining this transformation of the Mexican economy, it is important to keep in mind the historical difficulties that Mexico has suffered in its relationship with its powerful neighbor to the north. U.S. political intervention has taken many subtle (and not so subtle) forms.[15] Over the years, U.S. economic hegemony has been of constant concern as well. Even during the best of times, Mexico has been unable to diversify from a historical dependence on trade with the United States. The recent move toward Mexican economic openness and greater integration with the United States are all the more dramatic in light of Mexico's well-justified historical distrust of any relationship.

The proper pace of oil expansion became the subject of much debate within PEMEX, the government-run petroleum company, and within the state during the 1970s. A conservative approach, supported by popular opinion as well as by President Echeverría, viewed petroleum wealth as the nation's inalienable patrimony which must be fiercely protected against U.S. intervention. This group was sufficiently wary of U.S. pressure to expand production that they kept the vast oil discoveries of 1972 and 1973 a state secret until 1976. The Monterrey group–closely aligned with the most internationalized sector of domestic capital–favored the rapid expansion of production (Teichman 1988, 75).

The breakdown of the Bretton Woods system created instability in currency exchanges throughout the world. In its wake, this brought uncertainty and unpredictability to the management of Mexico's state-led development strategies. The U.S. recession and inflation problems of 1971 had a depressing effect on Mexico's economy. Finally, the 1973 oil crisis had a devastating impact on Mexico's balance of payments. In spite of a domestic oil industry, production levels had been insufficient to meet rising domestic demand in the 1960s, and Mexico had begun importing oil in 1971 just before international prices rose (Teichman 1988 50). The oil deficit reached a peak of over $250 million in 1974, but by 1975 Mexico was again exporting petroleum (Story 1986, 164).

State investment in public enterprises remained strong during the later years and diversified into many new industries. Hundreds of enterprises spanning a wide variety of activities were acquired by the state by the 1970s. Over the years of state-led growth, the expenditure on public enterprises increased by a factor of forty–from 822 million to 31,241 million (in 1960 pesos) by 1975 (Story 1986, 42). Compared with other Latin American countries, the state sector was small but included more of the larger industries and thus contributed to a concentration of industry. For instance, in the early 1960s the eleven largest business firms in the country were owned exclusively by the state. PEMEX, the national petroleum manufacturer remains one of the largest state-owned enterprises. Throughout the early 1970s, foreign investment was constrained and all new ventures were required to form joint operations (with domestic capital). Multinationals were active but also were concerned about the risk of property nationalization and an uncertain business environment.

The public provision of social goods expanded during the 1970s. The social security agency, IMSS, was revised in 1970 to extend care to many rural Mexicans, and child care centers were established for the children of female workers (Spalding 1981). In 1972, the Instituto Nacional del Fondo de la Vivienda para los Trabajadores (INFONAVIT), was established to provide worker housing through local unions. It was financed by a 5 percent employer contribution and a matching federal contribution. In its first ten years, 3.17 million low- and medium-cost units were constructed (Grayson 1989, 54). The expansion of the welfare state and the gendered consequences of its practices and policies did not survive the increased pace of internationalization in the third period of industrial growth, as we shall see in the next chapter.

Notes

1. Díaz's advisers, the *científicos*, provided social, economic, and political analysis to underpin the dictator's programs. Many were followers of the positivism of August Comte but others blended this philosophy with classical eco-

nomics and paternalistic and racist claims about the inferiority of the indigenous people. Emphasizing the modernization of Mexico and the pursuit of order and progress, the *cientificos* legitimated the dictatorship with the claim that "Mexico had to pass through a period of 'administrative power' before it could attain nationhood" (Meyer and Sherman 1991, p. 440).

2. Ownership makes forward and backward linkages in a vertically integrated firm, such that owners control the production of items that may be inputs to (or outputs of) their primary operations.

3. This account diverges from many historical accounts that emphasize the completely destructive character of the violent years of the Revolution. The debate over the impact of the Revolution on economic production is far from settled, but a revisionist account is beginning to suggest that capitalist production was in full swing before the Revolution and continued in many regions of the country during the conflict. For more details, see John Womack's (1978) comprehensive review of literature on this debate.

4. This assertion also runs counter to some historical interpretations which have claimed that the fundamental meaning of the Revolution lies in its repudiation of foreign interference in the economy (Womack 1978, p. 94).

5. The ascendance to power of the Sonoran military leaders General Alvaro Obregon and Plutarco E. Calles initiated the process of the creation of a more centralized state.

6. The dominant political party is now known as the Partido Revolucionario Institutional (PRI).

7. The Constitution promised state health care to citizens (who were not covered under IMSS) through the Secretaria de Salubridad y Asistencia (SSA) In what decade did SSA become a reality?

8. This was one of several development banks created in 1934.

9. Jesus Díaz de León earned his nickname as an enthusiast of Mexican popular rodeos (*charrería*). His forcible takeover of the railroad union offices in the late 1940s became know as the *charrazo*.

10. Based on the U.N. Economic Commission for Latin America (ECLA) post-World War II development strategy, the first stage of ISI involves substituting domestic commodities for imports in the consumer goods market. Mexico had been very successful in this sector, with domestic production supplying 93 percent of the market in 1965, climbing from only 65 percent in 1929 (Villareal 1990, p. 307). The second stage requires movement into the intermediate and capital goods markets.

11. In 1969, income inequality as measured by the Gini coefficient was 0.58 (Navarette cited in Cockcroft 1983, p. 188).

12. On the eve of the Mexico City Olympics, hundreds of thousands of students organized around democratic demands: the release of political prisoners and the reformation of law-enforcement agencies. Soldiers and police fired on an outdoor meeting, leaving several hundred dead and ending the movement.

13. An international agreement that was signed by major countries of the world in Bretton Woods New Hamphire in 1944 set up the the International Monetary Fund and a system of currency exchange rates that brought relative stability to major currencies from 1944 to 1971.

14. Special Drawing Rights (SDRs) are an artificial international reserve unit used to settle accounts among central banks. Created by the IMF in 1968, this new form of international liquidity signaled the beginning of the end of U.S. hegemony over the international monetary system.

15. For example, the Mexican-American War, which is popularly explained as "manifest destiny" in the United States, was in fact a devastating legacy when

seen from the Mexican perspective. School children in Mexico learn of the U.S. Invasion of 1846 to 1847 in which their country lost half its territory.

3

Internationalization and Privatization: Industrialization after 1976

> I see them all/wandering around/a continent without a name . .
> . all passing through Califas/enroute to other selves/and other
> geographies. (Guillermo Gómez-Peña 1996. *New World Border*,
> p. 2.)

Workers in contemporary Mexico face a decentralized production geography that marks a radical departure from the past. The previous concentration of industry in Mexico City played a pivotal role in the historical project of national political consolidation. In their efforts to centralize political power in the early twentieth century, post-revolutionary governments forged an alliance with the emerging industrial labor movement, while at the same time creating a comprehensive regulatory framework for labor relations. Through this state/worker alliance, political power and industrial capital coalesced in a densely concentrated geographical pattern. That is, post-revolutionary political leaders, bureaucrats, industrial workers, and capitalists were increasingly clustered in Mexico City. The political elites of this metropolitan center gradually overpowered provincial *caciques*[1] and as the federal bureaucracy expanded, industry was distilled into an analogous configuration centering on the capital city.[2] Workers in the formal sector (primarily males) enjoyed a mutually beneficial relationship with the state for several decades during which the unions ceded a measure of control to the corporatist state and in turn received secure jobs and adequate wages for their members. The state also provided many social benefits to workers and their families through such programs as the Mexican Institute for Social Security (a massive public health program) and, somewhat later, a housing program. During these years, union leaders were also powerful political actors, who frequently moved from labor union positions into elected and appointed government posts.

Since the mid-1970s, however, a new geography of production has emerged in Mexico that brings with it both new challenges and new possibilities for class and gender equity. As the old industrial geography of Mexico has been increasingly replaced by a new border-focused pattern, the former corporatist arrangements between the state and organized labor have begun to disintegrate. New arrangements between labor and the state are being forged in the border zone where the official unions have much less influence among workers and from which more radical unions may emerge. Likewise, new arrangements between men and women are being fashioned in households, in the workplace, and in official government practices and policies. These micro-scale class and gender struggles are occurring within the context of the reorientation of the state's development strategy–from a state-led industrial program of import substitution, to a neoliberal agenda that transforms the relationship between the workers and the state. The acrimonious nature of this new state/labor relationship has been co-evolving alongside the declining ability of the state to regulate capital flows (especially given pressure from the World Bank to deregulate the economy). At the same time there has been an increase in labor union organizing in both official and unofficial movements.

The historical transition from a state-led to a market-led industrial strategy has been facilitated by a geographical shift of industry from production sites centered around the capital to new sites at dispersed northern locations. A new factory regime in Mexico emerged in places that were remote from the influence of the powerful unions and entrenched industrial practices.[3] New relationships rapidly supplanted the previous model of capital accumulation and the coherent industrial policy which had undergirded that strategy. The speed with which the earlier factory regime was dismantled can be partly explained by geography. The far-flung northern sites made it difficult for union organizers to formulate a coherent strategy of resistance. Decentralized regulatory structures may have created additional barriers to collective action. And, the shifting allegiance of the Mexican state, which favored transnational corporations at the expense of official unions, weakened workers vis-à-vis their employers.

We can consider the three periods of Mexican industrial growth in terms of the state's alliance with domestic and foreign capital, the developmentalist "triple alliance."[4] In the late nineteenth century, foreign capital collaborated closely with the state but the state was the dominant partner. Since domestic capitalists were reluctant to invest in manufacturing, they had little impact in shaping the overall industrial effort. The state asserted its authority over foreign capital in the state-led period, yet it was careful to encourage (and monitor) foreign direct investment within many sectors of the economy. The state also acted to maintain existing domestic industrial investments (of the conglomerates) and to nurture a new group of industrial capitalists. But, in a marked departure from the past, the state has ceded its dominance to foreign capital in the years since 1976.

These shifting power relations have had a profound impact on the factory regimes of the three periods. Unions, labor rights, and state social provision were thus part of a regulated–and less harsh–state-led factory regime during the second period. The third period bears some resemblance to the first. The state has privatized most of its industrial assets and withdrawn from the active regulation of the employment relationship.

The Mexican industrial transition has involved a complicated set of interconnected social practices that are deeply but opaquely gendered. I have used the term "factory regime" as a shorthand way of acknowledging this complexity, which is summarized for the two factory regimes in Table 1.2. The Mexican state and the two comprehensive industrial systems it created were influenced by the gender and household arrangements that are depicted here in skeletal form. The economic transition was facilitated by a renegotiation of gender identities in the microcircuits of northern households, neighborhoods, and workplaces. The state also acted to gender the new factory regime in ways that would lower the costs of social reproduction (while keeping export products internationally competitive) and in ways that were distinct from the gendering of the old factory regime. Because the employers of the new factory regime are transnational corporations (TNCs), these findings also illustrate the ways in which contemporary transnational modes of capital accumulation are deeply gendered.

The gendered consequences of industrial expansion are particularly evident in the years after 1976. The "housewifization" that was prevalent in high growth sectors of the economy in the previous period gave way to female proletarianization in this period. The presumption of a universal male worker providing for his family no longer undergirds the dominant social and economic practices. Instead, women are the targeted employees in certain high growth sectors while youthful, healthy bodies of either sex are targeted in others. While workers in other industrial sectors are predominantly male, this fact no longer determines the course of national development.

The collective power of workers has been severely tested in the years after 1976. Workers can no longer count on their close affiliation with the state through the official labor unions. Some of these unions have been publicly disciplined as an example to the labor union movement that activism is no longer tolerated. Independent unions have struggled to make a difference against repressive acts coordinated by government officials, mainstream unions and private thugs. In countless other cases, an example of which we will see in chapter 5, official unions have undermined the interests and collective actions of their worker members. The old forms of workplace regulation, which constrained capitalist exploitation to some extent, have been dismantled. In their place there are new forms of regulation designed to maintain a good business climate and a quiescent workforce. Even if labor laws remain on the books, they are less actively enforced.

The Maquiladora Factory Regime

Close state/labor cooperation no longer exists in Mexico. A radical reorganization of the geography of production has had a salient impact on changing state/labor relations. Northern regions along the U.S.-Mexico border have attracted more new investment than the old industrial cores. Moreover, urban border sites have become a prototype for a new model of accumulation that underpins a new state development strategy. The continued northern pull of current investment is evident in the pattern of new business creation for 1992 (Figure 3.1). Some notable recent investments have been located in the interior cities of northern states. Within the sparsely populated northern regions of Mexico, new sets of labor relations reflecting the new state/labor relationship have been negotiated in dispersed factory sites that are remote from the influence of Mexico's labor unions. Many of the male and female workers in these new spaces were drawn from rural areas and were inexperienced in wage labor and collective bargaining. The older spaces, particularly the Mexico City agglomeration and the remote northern production site centered on Monterrey, continue to be significant industrial centers. However, the practices of the new production territories have been used subsequently to undercut the position of labor in these traditional production spaces.

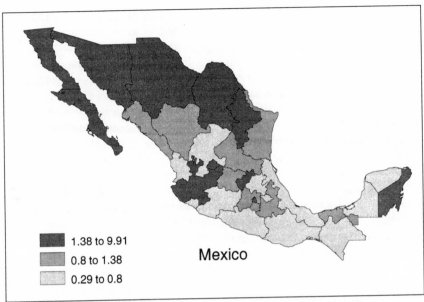

1.38 to 9.91

0.8 to 1.38

0.29 to 0.8

Mexico

Note: The values reflect the extent of deviation for the state's investment rate from the overall average.

Source: Pardo-Maurer and Rodríguez 1992.

Figure 3.1 Pattern of New Investment

Some institutional links from the old state/labor alliance do remain in place (e.g., the CTM's relationship to the Partido Revolucionario Institucional, PRI), but these connections have become tenuous and are certainly less beneficial for unions and workers than in the past. The state has aggressively singled out and disciplined dissident unions and union leaders, signaling a new antagonism to unionism and greater indifference to the concerns of workers. Other actions also illustrate the deterioration of this previously intimate arrangement: the loss of employment resulting from the privatization of state-owned enterprises; the state's effort to cultivate new sources of mass support through the community-based Solidarity Program;[1] and the supervision of national business and labor pacts that have effected devastating reductions in wages.

The best example of the reversal of the old development strategy is in the maquiladora sector, which originated as an ad hoc arrangement, but then quickly demonstrated a potential for rapid growth and for meeting a large share of the nation's foreign exchange needs. Several factors allowed maquiladora owners to devise new labor practices in this sector, a maquiladora factory regime. The owners first recruited a young, mostly female workforce that had little experience with waged work or with collective action. Second, the Mexican state did not actively encourage unionization in these new foreign-owned plants. Third, virtually all of the new production spaces were remote from the areas of entrenched labor unionism. Whereas the state's developmentalist logic during the ISI period had been to generate growth by increasing productivity, the goal of the current market-led period is to decrease the costs of social reproduction. This is seen clearly in the maquiladora sector where repression of labor keeps wages low. Moreover, low wages and poor conditions in the maquiladoras can be used to undercut the conditions and wages in other sectors and in other regions.

Geographical patterns of unionization within the maquiladora sector illustrate the way that space was used creatively by capital to create a new factory regime. Although there is some variation within the border zone, it must be emphasized that northern production practices are sufficiently distinct and homogenous to be considered a new entity (Table 1.2). The variability that does exist along the border reflects distinct historical divisions of labor in the region (Carrillo V. 1985; Williams and Passé-Smith 1991). With the exception of the east end of the zone, low unionization rates result from the recruitment of a youthful labor force to emerging industrial sites within the predominantly agricultural zone. Thus, at the far western end of the U.S.-Mexico border Tijuana has a 30 percent rate of unionization (1990) and is an important location of maquiladora investment with over 500 plants. And Ciudad Juárez, with the largest concentration of maquiladora employees in Mexico (129,000 in 1990), has only 13 percent unionization. At the eastern end of the U.S.-Mexico border, in contrast, the three cities in Tamaulipas have high rates of organization. Nuevo Laredo, the western-most of the three, has a 95 percent rate, while the labor force in both Reynosa and Matamoros is almost 100 percent organized. The high rates in Tamaulipas result from a history of entrenched labor union power that flourished there among petroleum workers. Workers at this end of the border have slightly better pay scales and better working conditions, but still nothing comparable to the working conditions under the earlier ISI factory regime.

This new state/labor relationship reflects the restructuring of the Mexican state, as it moved to dismantle its former comprehensive development policy and the import substitution industrialization project that had been its centerpiece. This ISI model had stimulated high growth rates for nearly forty years, but began to falter in the mid-1970s. Faced with an increasingly contradictory development strategy and escalating problems with international relations, the state abandoned the old ISI strategy. The state-led development program was replaced with a market-led neoliberal approach.

Labor unionists remain a sizable and important national force in the new era. Approximately ten million Mexican workers, nearly 35 percent of the total, are members of unions. During the 1980s, as Mexico was embracing a market-led model of development and becoming more integrated with the U.S. economy, these workers and their non-union counterparts saw their real wages decline precipitously. Real wages, which had already declined twenty percent from 1977 to 1982, declined an additional 66 percent between 1982 and 1990 (Cook 1993, 148; U.S. Congress 1993, 81). Tracing the geographical pattern of resistance to these changes is complex but enlightening. The shift in the terrain of conflict has weakened labor's collective strength during the neoliberal years, but the labor union movement may yet learn how to use new spaces to its advantage. Diffuse networks of collective strength may be less vulnerable to repressive actions. Worker solidarity that spans national borders and connects to community issues may be particularly resilient.

In addition to the wage declines of the 1980s and 1990s, workers witnessed an assault on labor unions that was coordinated by the state. Many of these anti-labor moves employed space creatively to undermine the strength of the labor union movement. One of these has been discussed above–the adoption of a new developmental model predicated on less–favorable labor relations practices in the new production regions of the north. A side-effect of the border industrialization program is that it has undermined old spaces of union control, while opening up a space for non-PRI militant unionism. In general, the rural agricultural population in these northern states had little previous experience with collective bargaining when they confronted their new transnational employers and therefore were, at least at first, ill-prepared to articulate and demand the satisfaction of their most basic needs.

A second anti-labor (and explicitly geographical) approach that the state adopted was to attack the centralized structure of the unions by attempting to destroy industry-wide contracts (*contracto ley*). Where this has been successful, it has effectively diluted the concentrated national power of unions that the state had previously encouraged. An example of this approach with far-ranging social implications was a 1992 agreement by the teachers union to decentralize not only their own union, but also the entire national school system (Cook 1995). A third strategy was to privatize and close major state-owned enterprises that contributed to "massive employment cuts and contract and work rule changes that . . . sapped the strength of Mexico's most important industrial unions" (Middlebrook 1995).

A fourth approach employed a familiar routine in state/labor relations but added a creative new twist. The familiar routine, known to all participants in Mexican politics, was to cultivate various groups of workers (usually in rival national organizations) and play them off against one another. This time the state developed a network of mass actors who were organized according to community and neighborhood membership, but *not* organized as workers. The community networks distributed social goods that were funded from massive capital accounts that had resulted from the sale of state-owned enterprises. The Solidarity Program (PRONASOL) targeted neighborhood, community, and rural networks where opposition parties were particularly strong. In this way, entire social networks of mass-based community support were created that could substitute for the traditional labor sector of the ruling party, the PRI. The political payoff was double: the strongholds of the opposition political parties were undermined, and the message was delivered to traditional labor unions that they were no longer an indispensable sector of the PRI.

A geographical perspective helps us understand the way these social struggles have evolved. North has been played against South; the center against the provinces; cores of labor union power have been disciplined and dismantled; and neighborhood groups have supplanted shop floor organizations. As workers have organized, they have encountered social barriers with complex spatial expressions.

Thus there has been a socio-spatial reorganization of social reproduction since 1976. Within high growth sectors, which serve as a prototype for development planning, social reproduction has been individualized. That is, workers must do many things for themselves that were previously provided by public programs. Wages are insufficient for workers to provide these goods and services to their spouses and dependents. This process induced a further fragmentation of families and households.[6] At the national level, social budgets have been slashed and social programs have been privatized. In a geographically uneven process, some social goods have been commodified while a small fraction of employers still provide a few previously socialized goods to their own employees (e.g., child care services).

The Neoliberal State and Industrial Promotion[7]

Industrial strategy in contemporary Mexico is based on a market-dominated neoliberal project of export promotion. Two manifestations of this dramatic and complete turnabout in development philosophy were Mexico's move to join the General Agreement on Tariffs and Trade (GATT) in 1986 and the 1994 North American Free Trade Agreement (NAFTA). The new growth model has entailed state retrenchment in many sectors of the economy, such as the privatization of social programs and state-owned industries. The state also has withdrawn from the active regulation of the employment relationship. However, in taking action to promote a few large national and international export producers, the state has retained a limited role in planning industrial strategy.

The most significant state intervention has been the direct provision of working capital to these export producers. Some exporters received as much as 50 percent of their capital needs from the state. To provide this assistance, Nafinsa and the Banco de Comercio Exterior (Bancomext) were given approximately 5 percent of the 1987 GDP—nearly $10.5 million (Cypher 1990, 184). Early in the 1980s, sector programs designed to choose the most promising industries began awarding tax holidays as well as rent and utility subsidies. In addition, the Programa de Fomento Integral de Exportaciones (Integrated Plan to Promote Exports, or Profiex) implemented four policies: (1) the permanent undervaluation of the peso; (2) the elimination of barriers to foreign exchange for exporters; (3) the simplification of import and export permits; and (4) a subsidy on the importation of machinery and equipment used in export manufacture. A group of only 100 national and international producers have been the principal beneficiaries of these policies (Cypher 1990).

The state abandoned its earlier efforts to limit foreign direct investment. The maquiladora sector provides one dramatic example of this reversal. Considered to be merely a regional solution at the time of its creation in 1965, the maquiladora program has become the exemplar of the latest factory regime. As it began to produce crucial flows of foreign exchange, it also became one of the fastest growing sectors of the economy.

The neoliberal project has both domestic and international support-ers. Since the early 1970s, the Mexican business elite had been calling for many of the changes seen today, especially the privatization of state enterprises. International pressure has come mainly in the form of policy-based lending by the World Bank and by the International Monetary Fund. The two institutions have enforced the other's lending criteria, in a sort of "cross-conditionality" (Cypher 1990).

International economic instability, the U.S. recession, and rising levels of class conflict in Mexico culminated in an overvalued Mexican peso and a loss of business confidence in the first half of the 1970s. As confidence fell, currency speculation in the form of capital flight sky-rocketed, reaching a level of $4 billion during 1976 (Ramírez 1989, 85). In 1976, the last year of President Echeverría's tumultuous term in of-fice, Mexico was forced to drastically devalue the peso from 12.5 to 19.7 pesos to the dollar. Along with the devaluation, Mexico implemented an IMF austerity program, designed to trim the national budget and re-duce the level of foreign borrowing.

Almost immediately, a long-simmering struggle within the state overturned the austerity program and switched to an expansionary pol-icy designed to increase petroleum production and exports. Overcoming a nationalistic group that feared U.S. intervention in the petroleum in-dustry, those who supported expansion argued that it would provide the solution to Mexico's economic problems. In his first month in office, President López Portillo aligned himself with this expansionary ap-proach by publicizing the scale of Mexico's proven oil reserves and an-nouncing plans to increase petroleum production.

Although many features of the state-led industrialization model remained intact, Mexico transformed its method of financing this style of development. Using oil wealth, the state began an ambitious pro-gram of public sector investment that included massive investment in the construction of infrastructure. The revived economy's specialization in oil production contributed to a rapid increase in both imports and the external debt (Villareal 1990, 299). Petrolization of the economy was accomplished very quickly, making Mexico the largest oil producing nation in Latin America and the sixth-largest in the world by the time of the second oil price shock in 1979. In a few years time, Mexico became overly reliant on exports from a single industry, earning as much as 75 percent of all foreign earnings through petroleum sales (Story 1986, 170; Cypher 1990, 108). In the late 1970s, the promise of rapidly increasing oil revenues made Mexico an attractive borrower, and the pace of for-eign lending increased.

The channeling of petroleum revenue to industrial promotion was made explicit in the 1979 National Industrial Development Plan, the state's first effort to weld its numerous industrial programs into one coherent policy. Clearly articulating regional and sectoral priorities, this document called for a growth rate of 7 percent in 1979, 9.5 percent in 1981, and 10.5 percent in 1982, all financed by petroleum earnings (Teichman 1988, 105). A complicated scheme of subsidized energy and petrochemical prices was included in the Industrial Development Plan. Within certain zones, new installations and expanding plants could receive as much as a 30 percent reduction in the cost of energy inputs (Story 1986, 178). Investment tax credits also were allocated according to the new regional and sectoral priorities (Story 1986; Cypher 1990).

Based on petroleum revenue and massive international borrowing, the Mexican financial boom of the late 1970s reshaped the domestic bourgeoisie by fueling speculative activity. The long-powerful conglomerates, the *grupos* who controlled diversified holdings in banks and industry, expanded rapidly and several new grupos were formed. The banking industry itself became increasingly concentrated. The number of banks fell from 240 in 1970 to 97 in 1981. The boom produced a polarization of the industrial sector in which large conglomerate owners used low-interest foreign loans to expand, while small and medium industrialists were forced to rely on expensive domestic credit (Maxfield 1990, 105).

The reorientation of the economy in the late 1970s proved unsustainable. Structural imbalances, continuous capital flight, balance of payment problems, and increased vulnerability to fluctuating global petroleum prices all converged to produce the devastating financial collapse of the early 1980s. The brief Mexican petroleum boom and the crisis that followed were both intricately connected to international processes. In the late 1970s, Mexico benefited from the rise in international petroleum prices, increased liquidity in global capital markets, and the lower interest rates offered by international banks competing to circulate their excess capital. By 1980, all of these same factors worked to Mexico's disadvantage. The price of crude oil and other commodities declined precipitously, capital markets shrank, and interest rates increased. When the industrialized countries entered the recession of the early 1980s, they turned to protectionism, undermining the export of manufactured goods coming from Mexico and other developing countries (Teichman 1988).

The petroleum boom deepened the contradictions internal to the state-led factory regime, even while the promise of increased oil revenues concealed them. The Mexican state, which had carefully sought to regulate foreign productive capital, and especially TNCs, found it-self tightly in the grip of international capital in the early 1980s.

The details of Mexico's economic breakdown are well known. In 1982, a severe Mexican liquidity crisis rocked the world's most secure financial centers. Unable to make the principal and interest payments on its foreign loans, Mexico's freewheeling deficit financing came to an abrupt end. The country's external debt had risen from $6 billion in 1970 to $86 billion in 1982 (Barry 1992, 83). Soon after the Mexican event, the problem became contagious: similar episodes were repeated throughout Latin America where the world's private banks, especially U.S. banks, had significant exposure.

Since the beginning of the debt crisis, Mexico has followed the or-thodox structural adjustment measures advocated by the World Bank, the IMF, and the United States: currency devaluation, trade liberal-ization, austerity, tax reform, and privatization. Moreover, the gov-ernment instituted its own program of wage and price controls in 1987, the Pacto de Solidaridad, to control the 160 percent inflation of that year.

The debt crisis of 1982 was a clear turning point in the decline of the power and relative autonomy of the Mexican state. One month after an-nouncing Mexico's inability to meet payments of the foreign debt, López Portillo, the out-going president, nationalized the nation's banks in a final effort to assert state authority over Mexican capitalists. His suc-cessor, Miguel de La Madrid Hurtado, worked to restore the power of financial elites by creating a stock exchange as a "parallel financial system" (Cypher 1990, 163). The strength of the bankers alliance was demonstrated by this incident (Hamilton 1986; Maxfield 1990). Ex-fi-nanciers were compensated for their losses, permitted in many cases to remain on bank management boards, and allowed to repurchase many or all of their former bank assets.[8] In addition, former bankers found a new venue for their speculative capital in the stock market. Both the 1983 reforms of the stock market and an increasingly liberalized foreign in-vestment policy contributed to a booming investment climate in the 1980s.

The most direct evidence of the decline of the state has been the scope of the privatizations of state-owned enterprises. Since 1983, many have been sold off, merged, or dissolved. At first this was a response to the debt problem and an effort to stabilize state finances. However, by 1985 the full-scale dismantling of the state economic sector was under-way. In the six years of the Miguel de la Madrid presidency (1982 to 1988), the government ordered the privatization of nearly 750 public enterprises. A total of nine hundred had been sold by 1991, leaving the state with about 260 firms.

Not only has the move toward privatization reduced the direct involvement of the state in the economy, but it also has concentrated more and more power in the hands of the financial-industrial grupos by facilitating the concentration of capital. Domestic conglomerates have been able to gain dominant or monopoly control in the following industries: copper, soft drinks, sugar and syrups, transport services, trucks and diesel motors, appliances, lumber and paper, and telecommunications (Barry 1992, 126).

The debt crisis reduced the capacity of the Mexican state to direct domestic economic policy. Rather than resisting the prescriptions of the United States, the IMF, and the World Bank, Mexico accepted many of the oppressive conditions attached to the loans that keep it afloat, and became a model debtor in the 1980s and 1990s. These conditions–reduced state expenditures, privatization of state-owned enterprises, currency devaluation, trade liberalization, reduced social spending–have reduced the state's relative autonomy from domestic and foreign capital.

When Mexico joined GATT in 1986, it broke with a long-standing nationalist development ethic. Earlier debates about the possibility of joining GATT had met with stiff resistance in 1979, leading to President López Portillo's decision to withdraw the proposal in 1980. Opponents had argued that opening Mexico's economy by reducing tariffs and eliminating import licenses would leave Mexico vulnerable to foreign manipulation. Above all, dissidents feared the possibility of U.S. intervention in the production and marketing of petroleum.

The question of GATT entry arose again after the 1982 debt crisis but remained an unpopular idea. Declining oil prices and continuing capital flight led to further economic decline in the mid-1980s which served to mollify the critics of economic openness. With minimal opposition, Mexico finally joined GATT in 1986 and proceeded to liberalize the economy by slashing tariffs and eliminating most import quotas and licenses. In less than a decade, Mexico moved from one of the most protected economies in the world to one of the most open (Barry 1992, 111).

For Mexico, the move to adopt GATT's trading guidelines was a crucial step toward building a dynamic *export*-oriented economy. In the 1980s Mexican state managers began to see the potential of increased economic integration with the United States as well as the liability of being left out of emerging regional trading blocks such as the European Union (EU) and the Canada/U.S. Free Trade Agreement (FTA). In 1987 and 1989, Mexico signed bilateral framework agreements with the

United States and in 1990 President Salinas formally proposed the creation of a more comprehensive U.S./Mexico free trade agreement.

Workers resisted the new factory regime and other consequences of these macroeconomic changes. In 1987, strikes by both the electrical and telephone workers were broken. Then a national petroleum workers' leader was forced from power in 1989. Meanwhile, government intervention during strikes in huge private workplaces (e.g., Modelo Brewery, Tornel Rubber, and the Ford Motor Company) revealed a new willingness on the part of the state to undermine worker movements (La Botz 1992).

In some respects NAFTA is a logical outcome of recent trends in Mexico. It is both a continuation of the 1980s liberalization of the economy and of increasing integration with the U.S. economy. Indeed, both of these movements have been accelerated and institutionalized by the agreement.

Ostensibly, Mexico's objective in pursuing NAFTA was to guarantee access to the U.S. consumer market (twenty-five times larger than Mexico's domestic market), since nearly two-thirds of Mexico's trade is with the United States. But Mexico's eagerness for large foreign capital inflows was a more fundamental motivation. Only such capital flows, especially in the form of direct foreign investment, could resolve the state's external sector problems. The maquiladora industry has been an exemplar in this regard, demonstrating the potential for U.S. investment in Mexico to yield increasingly large amounts of foreign exchange. NAFTA was a means with which to achieve new capital inflows that the 1989 debt reduction accord and the sweeping economic reforms of the 1980s had failed to attract.

The relative power positions of the members of dependent development's triple alliance have shifted during the third phase of industrial growth. The state has opted for a "new and more sophisticated form of dependent development," having relinquished its traditional guiding role in the economy to become "primarily a promoter and organizer of the transnational-dominated export program" (Alarcón and McKinley 1992, 86).

The Mexican economy has become both increasingly open and more integrated with the U.S. economy in the last two decades. As we have used the concept of dependent development in this chapter to examine some of the major turning points of this economic opening, the changing positions of the state, domestic capitalists, and foreign (mostly U.S.) capitalists become clear. Foreign capital has assumed the dominant role in this triple alliance through both increased lending and TNC production. On the other hand, the fortunes of the domestic bourgeoisie have been decidedly mixed. Many of the large financial-industrial grupos have benefited, while intense competition has squeezed smaller and medium capitalists, resulting in a rapid concentration of economic power. Clearly, the state has become the weakest element in the three-way partnership and its capacity for relative autonomy, given the movement of forces in the past decade, is almost nil.

The ascendance of the power of transnational capital (after 1976) has reduced the capacity of the state to lead industrial strategy, resulting in the current factory regime, more accurately termed the maquiladora factory regime. It is characterized by foreign direct investment, a weakened union movement, an unregulated work environment, and, as will be elaborated in chapter 5, state retrenchment in terms of social provision. This brief historical overview traces the contours of the changing factory regimes in twentieth-century Mexico but raises even more questions. How was the state able to reverse the terms of its social pact with labor? In what ways do the different factory regimes affect the daily lives of industrial workers? Did the recent transition to a maquiladora factory regime have finer-scale implications than this historical survey suggests? Did men and women experience the transition differently? The next three chapters will explore the ways in which the most recent factory regimes have evolved in specific locations.

Notes

1. The *caciques* were regional power brokers at various levels of authority, whose power rested upon patronage relationships with the landed class and others in their area.

2. Before the maquiladora program, the only sizable industrial investments outside the capital were: (1) a corridor stretching from Mexico City to Guadalajara; (2) Guadalajara; and (3) the more distant northern city of Monterrey.

3. The concept of "factory regime" is borrowed from Michael Burawoy (Burawoy 1985) and encompasses the apparatus of production regulation and the organization of production.

4. The coordination of local and international capitalists with the Brazilian state was termed a "triple alliance" in one of the first case studies to note the positive effect of a strong state policy on industrial growth. Brazil's "dependent development" was encouraged by an authoritarian military state that provided state subsidies, organized state-owned enterprises, and promoted corporate alliances (Evans 1979).

5. The Solidarity Program (PRONASOL) was initiated in 1988 by President Carlos Salinas de Gortari in order to rebuild the state's social base. Privatization funds were geographically targeted to community, neighborhood, and rural infrastructure projects.

6. Whereas the transition from phase 1 to phase 2 produced a nuclearization of family structure (in high-growth sectors), the transition from phase 2 to phase 3 prompted the individualization and fragmentation of family life.

7. Neoliberal policies are based on the liberalization of the economy toward a "free market" ideal. State intervention in most economic activities is seen as an anathema to those who would advocate neoliberal projects.

8. A distinction was made between investment banks and deposit banks, such that investment banks could be purchased, but a portion of the assets of deposit banks was protected against reprivatization.

4

The Old Model: A Case Study of State-Led Industrialization

> State building and labor mobilization during and after the Mexican revolution were interactive processes. The creation of new institutions to mediate labor-capital relations was an important element in the construction of the postrevolutionary state. (Kevin J. Middlebrook 1995. *The Paradox of Revolution*, p. 70.)

The years of state-led industrialization in Mexico (1930 to 1976) were characterized by the dominance of a strong state. Aligning itself with domestic and foreign capital in a comprehensive and ambitious project of import substitution, the state achieved such dramatic rates of growth that Mexico was held as an exemplar of successful Third World development.

This chapter examines the state-led factory regime that underpinned this success. A case study of Ciudad Madero, Tamaulipas, demonstrates that the remarkable achievements of these years rested upon accommodating the collective needs of labor through a variety of means. In the 1930s the working class was incorporated into the state apparatus through hierarchically organized and controlled labor unions. Labor rights were explicitly recognized and the state assumed the responsibility of enforcing these rights through the regulation of production. Since the 1940s, the state also has intervened in social reproduction–providing certain basic goods through state institutions set up for this purpose.

The social pact between labor and the state constrained the state to deal with labor and capital more evenhandedly than it had in the past.[1] Moreover, the industrial resources were not exclusively owned and operated by capital. The state itself undertook a project of direct production, after the dramatic oil and railway nationalizations in 1938 and 1937, respectively. In some cases these state-owned enterprises (SOEs) were located in strategic sectors but in later cases, they originated as private concerns that subsequently faltered and had to be rescued with state funds.

The state-led factory regime rested on and reinforced certain "traditional" notions of gender. The official labor unions that were incorporated into the state were almost exclusively male. Thus, production relations were understood to be between male workers and capital, or male workers and the state, in the case of state-owned enterprises. Elements of social provision (e.g., health care, housing, education, social services, and child care) within the factory regime, on the other hand, were to be extended to the worker and his dependents, i.e., wife and children. It will become apparent later in the comparison with the contemporary maquiladora factory regime that these gendered assumptions affected household formation, among other things.

The state-led factory regime was a regional phenomenon; it developed in the large urban areas of central Mexico, especially Mexico City, Guadalajara, and Monterrey. These cities with their well-developed infrastructures and abundant labor supplies appealed to early industrial capitalists.

This chapter describes the local operation of the state-led factory regime in order to understand how and why the state pursued this particular strategy. Specifically, how and why did the state become active in social reproduction? What forms did social provision take? What happened to this factory regime in the recent period of internationalization and privatization? What have been the consequences for industrial workers and how have they responded?

Ciudad Madero, Tamaulipas

Due to its long history of unionization within private and public industries, Ciudad Madero, Tamaulipas, is representative of the communities shaped by Mexico's program of state-led industrialization. Labor militancy in these places, in turn, produced the mix of elements that gave rise to a prosperous expanding factory regime in mid-century. Named for late president Francisco I. Madero whose "anti-reelection campaign" had catalyzed revolutionary sentiment against the dictator Porfirio Díaz, Ciudad Madero was also closely associated in the popular mind with labor activism. A man who was once rejected for a job in Monterrey because he was from Ciudad Madero said that the city's reputation had cost him an excellent career opportunity. His potential employers explained to him that it was well known that "babies were born in Ciudad Madero with a copy of 'La ley federal de trabajo' (Federal Labor Law) in their hands" and thus were a bad risk as employees (Salcedo, personal interview, July 25, 1992).[2]

Local factories were in place at the beginning of the period of state-led industrialization and significantly increased production and employment levels throughout these years. A mix of publicly, privately, and cooperatively owned factories in the city has employed a large percentage of the workforce throughout the twentieth century. In 1990, a total of 29 percent of all the employed people in Ciudad Madero were occupied in manufacturing (INEGI, *Censo General de Población* 1990b).

The contemporary city of Ciudad Madero is squeezed between two other populous communities: Tampico, a major and historical Gulf of Mexico port; and Altamira, a rapidly expanding commercial and industrial center. The city is physically constrained on all sides with Tampico and Altamira forming a barrier on the north and west side of the city and the Gulf of Mexico and the Panuco River forming a barrier to the south and east (Figure 4.1).

The region was originally inhabited by the Huastec Indians and the coastal site of present-day Ciudad Madero/Tampico attracted early and permanent Spanish settlers when a mission was established by Fray Andrés de Olmos in 1532 (Anaya Nieves 1974). Life along the gulf coast was subject to occasional invasions of pirates and competing imperial powers. Even after independence in 1829, Tampico residents evacuated the city when it became the site of the last battle between Mexico and the Spanish forces attempting to reconquer the colony. Later, in 1866, Tampico was one of several cities recaptured from the short-lived French Empire in Mexico as the country struggled to regain its independence.

The particular site that became Ciudad Madero was well known in the nineteenth century for a traveler's inn and restaurant which was run by a woman named Doña Cecilia Villareal. Her inn also operated a ferry across the River Panuco allowing men and pack animals to head south into the present-day state of Veracruz (*Los Municipios de Tamaulipas* 1988). As a result, the town was variously referred to as "Villa de Cecilia," "Doña Cecilia," "Meson," and "El Paso de Doña Cecilia." (Anaya Nieves 1974, 59; Fuentes 1974, 83; Trujillo y Núñez 1974, 25; Infante 1991, 15). In 1930, six years after the city of Villa

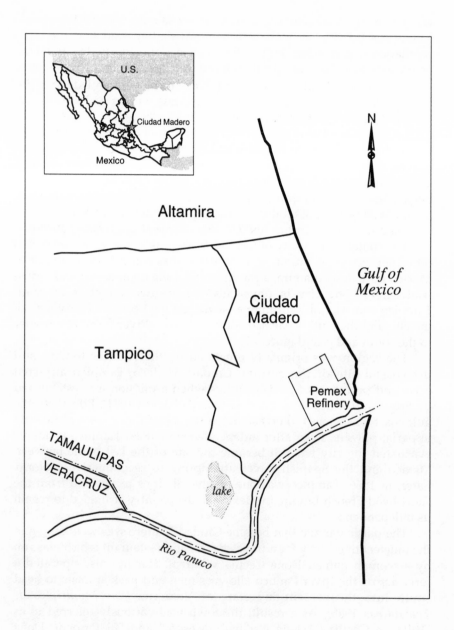

Figure 4.1 Ciudad Madero, Tamaulipas

Cecilia had established its political autonomy from Tampico, the name was changed to honor the man who had shaped the early thrust of the Mexican Revolution (Los Municipios de Tamaulipas 1988, 50).

Oil and the refining of oil have been central to the economy of Ciudad Madero in the twentieth century. The Pierce Refinery opened for production in 1897 (Silattum 1974, 30) only to be surpassed by "the largest and most modern refining plant in Mexico" constructed by Royal Dutch Shell in 1919 (Middleton 1919, 43). Rapid expansion of the oil industry, driven by the World War I increase in petroleum demand, is clearly the reason for an increase in population in Tampico from 9,000 residents in 1900 to 100,000 residents in 1922 ("Epoca del Auge Petrolero en Tampico" 1988, 42).

Although Tamaulipas was not a major center of Revolutionary unrest, its history does illustrate the way in which regional power-brokers used reform movements after the struggle to consolidate local power. These local *caudillos* mobilized whatever constituencies they could to assert a transitory form of authority as the central power struggled to exercise authority over the states. By the mid-1930s the *caudillos* were assimilated into the bureaucratic structure they had helped to create (Fowler Salamini 1990).

In Tamaulipas, an agrarian state dominated by a hacienda system of production, these caudillos typically aligned themselves with wealthy landowners. However, they also pursued land reforms when it became politically expedient to do so but confined their impact to areas of significant peasant mobilization. Large portions of the northern and southern parts of the state remained untouched. The caudillos slowly came to recognize the potential of urban workers in Tampico as well. César López de Lara, governor of the state from 1920 to 1923, aligned himself with the moderate union of stevedores, Gremio de Alijadores, but eschewed a relationship with the more radical oil workers. By 1925 his successor Emilio Portes Gil found both unions as well as a peasant league he organized to provide a more powerful political base (Fowler Salamini 1990).

In spite of an increasing labor militancy, the Tampico/Ciudad Madero local economy prospered during the 1920s and 1930s as oil production levels rose steadily. Population levels skyrocketed again during World War II when recruiters, responding to a boom in oil demand, scouted interior regions and offered free traveling expenses to new petroleum workers and their families. Many of these new workers quickly sold their land and farm animals for minimal prices and arrived in Ciudad Madero full of hope for their future good wages and wealth (Infante 1991).

Local Industries

Massive petroleum refineries have been the backbone of the Ciudad Madero economy in the twentieth century. However, there are, and have been, other small and medium-sized industries. The largest of these is Química del Mar, a privately owned processing plant for magnesium oxide. Most of the other industries originated as projects of the petroleum workers union, although at least one of these now operates as a private clothing producer.

As already noted, the growth of the city was clearly a result of the expanding oil production. Because of the ocean port and the proximity of many oil wells, Tampico became an important administrative center as well for British, Dutch, and U.S. oil companies. The portion of Tampico that later became Ciudad Madero was an industrial zone for these foreign enterprises, providing locations for refining and storage. The largest of these operations were Compañía Mexicana de Petróleo El Aguila (now Refinery Madero) and *Pierce Oil Company* (now Refinery Arbol Grande) ("Epoca del Auge Petrolero en Tampico," 1988, 42).

The workers in El Aguila refinery organized a union in 1923 and went on strike the following year in a disagreement over working conditions ("Documentos Históricos" 1988, 55). Such disputes were common in this and other local plants during the next fifteen years. These ongoing problems contributed to a struggle between foreign oil companies and the newly formed Mexican government over the rights to petroleum (Story 1986).

Labor strife at these plants illustrates the pressure that the Revolutionary mobilization of popular sectors had brought to bear upon the new government. After the Revolutionary War, strikes and other labor struggles were constant reminders of the increased strength of labor. This rising militancy goes a long way toward explaining the inclusion of labor in the state apparatus as a part of its corporatist structure in the 1930s.

A dispute between Mexico and the United States over the right to petroleum coincided with these labor struggles. Although the Mexican Constitution of 1917 had provided the legal basis for the nationalization of this important resource, the United States applied

economic, political and military pressure on Mexico during the 1910s and 1920s, which included two invasions, the dispatch of a private army of 6,000 into the oil region, and ongoing threats of invasion. (La Botz 1992, 102)

Despite these threats, the conflict between labor and capital led to the dramatic nationalization of the holdings of seventeen oil companies on March 18, 1938, by decree of President Lázaro Cárdenas. The conflict had escalated when an arbitration board granted an increase in wages and an improved pension and welfare system to petroleum workers after a prolonged strike. The foreign companies refused to obey the board as well as the Mexican Supreme Court that ruled in support of the board's decision. After the nationalization, numerous small unions organized into a national union, Sindicato de Trabajadores Petroleros de la República Mexicana, (STPRM) (Roxborough 1984).

The local branch of the oil workers union in Ciudad Madero is Section Number One of the STPRM. These workers, along with workers elsewhere, are employed by the state-run oil company Petróleos Mexicanos, (PEMEX). Throughout the period of state-led growth in Mexico, and in less extreme form today, these two institutions–the STPRM and PEMEX–had a profound impact on the local economy and daily life. Both productive relations and social reproductive ones were organized by these two intertwined enterprises. As one retired worker put it, "We were autonomous. Everything was controlled by the union" (Infante Alvarez, personal interview, July 29, 1992). Under the surveillance and guidance of PEMEX and STPRM, the family, the household and the community were bound more tightly to the Mexican state (i.e., through the provision of necessary social reproductive goods such as health care, child care, and education). The state-led factory regime was typified by the institutionalization of productive and social reproductive relationships.

The collective strength of workers in Ciudad Madero is evident in the many ways the STPRM has taken action to shape the community to suit workers' needs. One example is the formation of small and medium industries conceived and operated by the oil workers union that were in operation until 1989. Ten or more industries as well as consumer cooperatives were run by the union and have their origins in the 1940s when PEMEX lent money to workers to encourage their formation (Randall 1989, 106). In Ciudad Madero, these small industries and consumer cooperatives grew dramatically in the late 1950s and remained strong until the late 1980s. However, when several union leaders were jailed and the union forcibly restructured in 1989, most of these entities were sold. The industries included: clothing; chemicals and soap; steel rebar; workshop for steel windows, doors, and tanks; furniture; and screws

(Alonso Morales, personal interview, July 28, 1992; "Plan Lázaro Cárdenas," 1988).

Although these small and medium-sized factories were profitable enterprises, they were developed in order to meet the needs of the Ciudad Madero community. The fact that a labor union had enough money to subsidize the creation of such activities demonstrates the collective strength of some elements of labor during the state-led factory regime. The clothing factory, which is typical of these union-run industries, employed eighty people during the thirty years in which it was a STPRM-run cooperative. It originally produced work clothing for PEMEX workers throughout Mexico and later began to stitch school uniforms as well. In local publications, the founders proudly proclaimed that their goal was to create more jobs as well as to relieve the burden of the cost of work clothes on families ("Plan Lázaro Cárdenas" 1988). Today the factory, one of the few still in operation, is private and has thirty full-time workers.

Along with state-owned enterprises and small cooperatives, medium-sized private industries have been in operation in Ciudad Madero for many years. One of the largest of these, the magnesium oxide factory Química del Mar began operation in 1967 to process material extracted from the ocean floor into a form usable for producing refractory fire bricks. The pellet-shaped product is shipped to another factory, owned by the same conglomerate, to make the fire bricks.

The Ciudad Madero plant has maintained a workforce of nearly 200 people through the years (Rodríguez González, personal interview, July 30, 1992). Hiring only males for the manufacturing positions, Química del Mar is a private company that is wholly owned by one of the largest of the large Mexican conglomerates, Servicios Industriales Peñoles, S.A. de C.V. These privately employed workers have been unionized since the opening of the factory. They are members of the Sindicato de Trabajadores de la Industria Petroquímica y Carboquímica, having their own local, Section Eight of Química del Mar (Molina Flores, personal interview, July 23, 1992).

In the state-led factory regime, the state explicitly limited the power of private employers, such as Química del Mar in several ways. First, industrialists were not free to set the terms under which they dealt with labor. Second, the state acted to promote and subsidize certain industries, distorting the market environment. And third, the state itself directed industrial enterprises, introducing further distortions and changing the terms of labor relations by setting an independent example. Química del Mar, like other large private employers during the years of state-led growth, accepted labor unions as legitimate representatives of the workers.

Strong unions have been important to Ciudad Madero workers, whether they were employed in private or public industry. During the years of state-led growth, the unions enjoyed the recognition and support of the state. In turn, their strength led to the reorganization of social reproduction, through the direct state provision of particular goods.

Social Provision

A fundamental element of the state-led factory regime was the state provision of certain basic goods and services to workers. This provision was a result of the same ongoing struggles that led to incorporation of the labor unions into the state apparatus. The guarantee of such important goods as health care was a response to labor militancy but at the same time it served to insure the continued loyalty of those on the receiving end.

Social provision within the state-led factory regime was conceived as a support for workers and their families. Because the workers in the official labor unions of the 1930s and 1940s were overwhelmingly male, this had certain gendered consequences that will become more apparent in the comparison with the maquiladora factory regime. For now, a more general example will demonstrate that the state-led factory regime is constructed upon a notion of a male worker supporting a nuclear family. The federal social security program (IMSS), which began in 1943, guarantees health care to a worker and *his* dependents, defined as *his* wife and children.

There are two main channels of social provision in Ciudad Madero. First are the federal programs such as social security, IMSS, and the worker's housing fund, INFONAVIT. Second are the social programs of the petroleum workers' union, which, since 1959, have been coordinated through the Grupo Unificador Revolucionario Nacionalista y Humanista (GURNH). The GURNH expanded quickly from a savings bank to a comprehensive set of social programs that touched every aspect of community life: hospital and health clinics, schools, child care centers, grocery and department stores, small industries, recreational facilities, repair shops, agricultural experiment stations, and street paving crews. Because of the extent of GURNH's programs, they are crucial for PEMEX households. "The union even takes care of us when we die," says Alfredo Valdés, explaining that several generations of

Ciudad Madero's citizens have been buried by a cooperatively owned and PEMEX-subsidized funeral parlor employing fifteen people (Valdés, personal interview, July 29, 1992). Many social reproductive activities that might have been performed by individuals or by households have been organized within the community, that is, they have been socialized. This has had a clear impact on the quality of life in the community, even for those not employed at PEMEX. Because this reorganization of social reproduction is so complete, the programs have overlapped and overshadowed federal social programs for PEMEX employees and their eligible family members (Grayson 1980; 1989; Briseño 1988, 67).

The money for these union cooperatives and social programs (i.e., clinics, childcare centers, repair shops, street paving) came largely from PEMEX itself, although workers were required to contribute 2 percent of their earnings. Money from PEMEX was assessed each time the state-owned company contracted with a private enterprise, often U.S. companies, for specific goods or services. For most operations PEMEX was required to pay only 2 percent to the union fund, however for contracts such as drilling operations the fee was 40 percent (Corro and Reveles 1989; Randall 1989). In addition to these sources, GURNH has also been financed by corrupt practices such as the selling of jobs and the manipulation of contracts (Grayson 1980, 90).

Much has radically changed in the years since 1989, when the union leader Joaquin Hernández Galicia was jailed on charges of "corruption and gangsterism." Known everywhere as La Quina,[3] the leader's arrest in Ciudad Madero marked the state's deliberate effort to crush the independent power of the STPRM, while preserving its hierarchical structure. Some of the implications for families were widespread and immediate. "We lost the neighborhood stores where we had always bought goods at reduced prices," Alfredo Valdés reflected, speaking of the forty-five stores operated by STPRM that had provided a 20 to 25 percent discount (Valdés, personal interview, July 29, 1992). These stores, which had become an integral part of daily life for most families, and several other union functions were privatized shortly after La Quina and some fifty of the unions' officers and employees were jailed.

The discipline imposed on the union reflected the conclusion of a political struggle within the state over the privatization of state-owned enterprises (SOEs). La Quina and his own powerful national organization had supported a group within the PRI that opposed the sale of SOEs. When the pro-privatization candidate Salinas de Gortari won the struggle and was inaugurated as president, he immediately organized a joint military and police raid on STPRM and its insubordinate leader. The state asserted its authority over the union by imposing new leadership: expelling 10,000 technical and professional workers from the union; laying off thousands of casual workers; and rewriting the collective bargaining agreements (La Botz 1992).

This federal action and subsequent reorganization of the industry has challenged the independent power of the union, which was manifest in the social programs among other things. The programs that have survived have much smaller budgets and are now administered by a union office titled simply, Prevision Social, or social provision. Only very basic programs have survived. They include: a child care center that is available for the children of any female PEMEX worker; and the provision of health care by a large "Regional Hospital," a 24-hour clinic, and a smaller clinic. Services are provided by these institutions to 60,280 Madero residents of which about 12,000 are workers and the others are dependents (Ramírez Quijano 1992). In spite of their losses, workers and residents alike continue to assert the belief that their government and their employers owe them a certain quality of life. "We have the right to take our children to the PEMEX child care center," Maria Teresa Medina stated simply, when I asked her who took care of her children (Medina, personal interview, July 30, 1992).

The state-led factory regime involved a particular organization of social reproduction. The federal guarantee and provision of health care to workers and their families established a channel in 1943 for direct social provision that was the material basis for a new social-reproductive relationship between the state and workers.

A strong Mexican state has produced a century of uneven industrial progress. In the early years of this process, during the dictatorship, the industrialists were virtually indistinguishable from the state. Industrial capital was highly concentrated and the structure of production was noncompetitive. In the "miracle years" of state-led growth (1930 to 1976), the power of the industrialists remained strong but was limited by state efforts to incorporate sectors of the working classes into the ruling party and the state through the provision of social benefits and the encouragement of state-sponsored unions.

The Ciudad Madero case study demonstrates the many ways in which the state was active in social reproduction during the 1940s, 1950s, and 1960s in Mexico. Direct provision (from the federal government to individuals) was channeled through IMSS health care plans and INFONAVIT housing programs. A more complicated but direct state provision was funneled through the state-owned enterprise PEMEX and STPRM, its union affiliate, which provided a comprehensive health plan and a housing plan, as well as schools, libraries, and daycare centers for the community. Besides these activities, the state actively supported unions and workers in their struggle for good working conditions and livable wages. These state interventions translated into more political power and a better standard of living for workers during the state-led period of industrialization.

The changes in Ciudad Madero production in recent years underscore the ascendance of the power of capital and the decline of the state-led factory regime. In contrast to the historical model, production relationships in places and regions dominated by the maquiladora factory regime illustrate the embrace of a neoliberal free-market approach to development.

Notes

1. The social pact between the state and labor was a product of the Mexican Revolution (1910 to 1920) in which worker-organized "red Battalions," although fairly insignificant to the outcome, did demonstrate the potential importance of urban and industrial workers as political allies. The postrevolutionary leadership developed an administrative and legal framework to regulate production as part of its sustained effort to centralize political power. Simultaneously, they sought an alliance with the emerging industrial labor movement (Middlebrook 1991).

2. The names of industrial workers throughout the book have been changed to protect their anonymity.

3. When used in reference to a person, this term for cinchona bark or quinine implies a horrible or nasty personality.

5

The New Model: A Case Study of the Maquiladora Industry

> At the end of the seventies, but especially beginning with the economic crisis of 1982, the neo-conservative trends that reduce the size of the state and end the developmentalist policies of modernization bring Mexico closer to the situation in the rest of the continent. (Néstor Garcia Canclini 1995. *Hybrid Cultures: Strategies for Entering and Leaving Modernity*, p. 61.)

A new factory regime emerged in the northern border region of Mexico in the mid-1960s that matured to typify the period during which industry was both internationalized and privatized. The evolution of the maquiladora industry in Nogales, Sonora, gives us a close-up look at the way the new factory regime affected the lives and relationships of people in northern Mexico.

The organization of social reproduction within the household is one aspect of these changing relationships. Large numbers of women working in maquiladoras transformed the gender relations in the factory as well as in the home. Unlike the previous industrial model in which a single male wage earner sustained a nuclear or even extended family, workers in the new regime often reconstitute the household in order to pool two or more factory wages. In some cases the principal breadwinners of the family are the children of these households: sixteen- and seventeen-year-old maquiladora workers. These changes impact workers' ability to restore themselves on a daily basis and nurture the next generation of workers. Social reproduction is not, however, confined only to the household. The Mexican state has been active in social reproduction during the twentieth century through programs of universal education, socialized health care and child care, and state-funded housing.

Decentralization and devolution of labor union power through the geographical balkanization of labor regulation characterizes the new factory regime. Localized regulation of labor conflicts has worked to the disadvantage of efforts to engage in regional or national organizing in the northern regions, similar to the local operation of the National Labor Relations Board in the United States (Clark 1989). In the new factory regime, each labor grievance must proceed through the bureaucratic layers of newly decentralized regulatory structures. The fact that these layers are widely dispersed in space creates an additional restraint for workers, who must assemble sufficient resources to cover transportation expenses and forgo regular incomes in order to travel and pursue an appeal beyond the immediate locality. Unsympathetic arbiters in the neoliberal years have made these geographical barriers all the more potent such that local worker issues tend to be confined to small geographical and jurisdictional units.

Nogales, Sonora, is a typical northern industrial city, exhibiting many hallmarks of the new factory regime (Table 1.2). Workplace control is asserted by individual factory managers who reinforce their individual strengths by harmonizing the practices of larger factories. Collaborating through the Nogales Maquiladora Association, local managers keep a downward pressure on wages and benefits, while minimizing inter-factory competition for labor. Thus, most maquiladora workers earn the minimum wage, which has now come to be an individual wage in the new factory regime. Although workers change jobs frequently, they find that this action provides little leverage for improvement in such a tightly controlled context. Furthermore, a large percentage of workers in the local labor market rely on maquiladora incomes. An elaborate system of "bonuses" (which are actually an *essential* part of the wage) disguises the fact that this minimum is hardly a living wage for an individual. To survive, many workers create extended households in which they pool multiple factory wages, or live temporarily in company-run single-sex dormitories. Nogales' corporate dormitories are an unusual feature of the new factory regime and, for this reason, will be discussed separately in the next chapter. Suffice it to say for the moment that the Nogales dormitory system–while only sheltering a few thousand workers–allows for greater flexibility and profitability for the transnational employers operating in the city. In contrast to the old factory regime where workers may retire with 100 percent pay after 35 years of service, jobs in Nogales are insecure. Job turnover rates in 1992 averaged fifteen to sixteen months. Transnational employers experiment with quality circles and other new techniques of workplace control.

Several of the largest factories have union contracts, but these function as protection against genuine collective bargaining, as described below. The local reorganization of social provision has increased the power of the employer in Nogales. This is because many social goods that were abundantly provided by the state in the old factory regime are only available through the employment relationship in Nogales. Workers thus are less able to challenge employers, because they rely on their jobs for these essential social goods.

Changes in the regulatory environment in Nogales also reflect the enhanced power of employers. The lax enforcement of labor laws includes such things as the employment of underage workers, wage payments below the legal minimum, firings without compensation, and the disregard for occupational health regulations. At the same time, every effort is made to contain local labor grievances so they do not proceed to another jurisdiction. The state itself uses the decentralized regulatory structure of the Conciliation and Arbitration Boards (where grievances are filed and adjudicated) to spatially contain worker discontent and suppress labor unrest. Maquiladora owners and managers share information and blacklist individuals who have filed grievances or initiated protests. All of these various measures work together to produce an environment of intimidation and insecurity that makes genuine collective action extremely difficult.

A brief history of Nogales, below, is followed by an account of the evolution of the maquiladora industry in the region. We then turn to new processes of social provision connected to this new factory regime and an enumeration of health hazards associated with maquiladora employment in Nogales, and by implication, throughout the maquiladora zone.

Nogales, Sonora

Framed by the contentious relationship of two vastly unequal nations, the community of Nogales, Sonora, is an artifact of Mexico's northern border with the United States. No settlement existed when the 1853 Gadsden Purchase imposed a new international boundary between the U.S. territory of New Mexico[1] and the Mexican state of Sonora. Even in 1882, when U.S. and Mexican railroads were joined in a narrow canyon passageway along an old, well-worn trade route from the Pacific Ocean port of Guaymas, Sonora to Tucson, Arizona, there were only a handful of residents. *Nogales*, meaning "walnuts" in Spanish, was the name adopted by the merchant communities on both sides of the border: Nogales, Arizona, and Nogales, Sonora.

The U.S.-built railroads, approved by dictator Porfirio Díaz in the late nineteenth century, transformed the Sonoran economy while linking it to the U.S. economy. The railroad physically connected Sonora to Arizona and facilitated a regional economy based on commercial agriculture and large-scale mineral extraction. Tracks were not extended to the populous central highlands of Mexico. Nogales expanded as local merchants began to provide supplies and machinery for regional mining operations. International trade and smuggling were important elements of the Nogales economy from its beginning. The city has become a significant port of entry for produce for the U.S. market, providing nearly one-half of winter fruits and vegetables in recent years.

As a border city, Nogales has long been a destination for Mexicans seeking to find work in the United States. Beginning in World War II, those seeking work in the United States were granted temporary permission through the bilateral Bracero Program of contract labor. A bracero center operated in Nogales, processing thousands of Mexicans (almost exclusively male) to work as seasonal agricultural laborers in the United States. Designed to alleviate U.S. labor shortages, the program was unilaterally canceled by the United States in 1964. Termination of the Bracero Program and the consequent high rate of unemployment at Mexico's northern border were two of the factors contributing to Mexico's industrialization of its northern border.

The 1965 Mexican Border Industrialization Program, also known as the maquiladora or "twin plant" program, dramatically changed the local economy in most U.S.-Mexico border cities, including Nogales. The Mexican federal program encouraged foreign industrial investment through the use of government subsidies and new regulations that granted manufacturers duty-free importation of machinery, parts, and raw material. At the same time, changes in the U.S. tariff schedule made it cost effective for U.S.-based transnationals to assemble goods overseas for the U.S. market. As products flowed back to the U.S. consumer market, import duties were charged only on the value added (usually labor costs). U.S.-owned manufacturers, particularly electronics assembly operations, opened factories employing Mexican laborers in Nogales, Sonora. This industry expanded rapidly to become a significant sector of the local economy. People now migrate from rural Sonora and other parts of Mexico to work in the factories.

Nogales, Sonora, has always dwarfed its neighbor Nogales, Arizona. When many people of Mexican origin were repatriated to border cities in Mexico during the depression of the 1930s, this urban asymmetry was accelerated. The 1992 population of Nogales, Sonora, is approximately 250,000, overshadowing it U.S. counterpart of 25,000.

The Maquiladora in Nogales

Early Industrialization

Governor Luis Encinos and the state of Sonora initiated a concerted effort of industrial promotion several years before the federal maquiladora program. With a 1962 state law, *Ley no. 16*, Encinos established local promotion committees in three Sonoran border communities: Nogales, Agua Prieta, and San Luis Río Colorado. In addition, the law offered complete tax exemptions to new industries for ten years and a refund of up to 50 percent for the following five years. Between 1962 and 1966, 102 industries took advantage of this law. It should be noted that these small factories entailed small investments. For example, one electronic component manufacturer, COMCO, employed eighteen workers in Nogales in 1963 with a total initial investment of $500 (Ramírez 1988, 48). The governor also extended the free zone status of Nogales and Agua Prieta for four years. This status, which allows the tariff-free importation of consumption goods to certain Sonoran border regions, had been periodically renewed since the 1930s.

These efforts were strengthened in 1965 by the federal maquiladora program, which was designed to attract foreign investment and alleviate unemployment along Mexico's northern border. The federal program and its many subsequent revisions created the appropriate conditions for the new factory regime. In 1967, the multinational electronics firm Motorola established the first maquiladora in Nogales. Company spokespeople praised the maquiladora program and boasted that lower wages in Mexico would save the corporation $4 million dollars annually (*Arizona Daily Star* November 15, 1971). In addition, governor Félix Serna and the state of Sonora granted Motorola a ten-year exemption from all taxes in an effort to attract large U.S. companies (Orantes 1987, 21). The venture was successful and Motorola quickly expanded. Only two years later, at the dedication of a new $240,000 building, Arizona governor John R. Williams hailed the event as another link connecting the economies of Arizona and Sonora (*Arizona Republic* June 22, 1969).

The maquiladora program grew rapidly in Nogales after Motorola arrived. By 1970, it had been joined by other Fortune 500 companies such as Packard Bell and Magnavox (Orantes 1987, 21). In 1971, Motorola alone had 1,000 local workers while thirty factories throughout the city employed a total of 4,800 Mexican workers (*Tucson Citizen* September 13, 1971).

The Industrial Park

The establishment of a 116-acre industrial park south of Nogales accelerated the expansion of the maquiladora industry (Figure 5.1). This park and many others in the border states were the result of cooperation between officials at various levels of the government and foreign entrepreneurs. The state often makes special land leasing arrangements and provides such infrastructure as deep wells, communications systems, and fuel and energy networks. Government officials were willing to provide these subsidies after they observed that large industrial investors favored industrial parks. The state of Sonora currently has twenty-four industrial parks, half of which are government run and half privately owned.

A U.S. businessperson, Richard Campbell, developed the Nogales industrial park in partnership with Richard Bolin, a U.S. industrial consultant. Campbell had previously been active in the export of commercial produce from Mexico and had set up his own factory in Nogales to build shipping crates for his produce. In 1963, two years before the maquiladora program, he petitioned the Mexican government for permission to establish an industrial park in Nogales to expand his operations (*Arizona Republic* October 17, 1971). His partner Richard Bolin was a manager at Arthur D. Little de Mexico (ADL), an industrial consulting firm specializing in economic development. Bolin decided to invest in Campbell's industrial park after conducting a study commissioned by the Mexican government that demonstrated the potential for industrial development along the U.S.-Mexico border. It was during the course of this research that Bolin claims he originated the idea of maquiladoras (Sklair 1989, 43).

With the consent of the city administration, Sonoran governor Encinos responded to Campbell's development plans by expropriating 60 hectares for the industrial park (Ramírez 1988). In 1969, 46 hectares of this property was leased by the city to La Sociedad Mercantil Parque

Industrial de Nogales, SA de CV (PINSA), a group that included Campbell and Bolin. PINSA assured the city that it would promote the park among U.S. industrialists and complete an expansion of the park by 1973 (Ramírez 1988, 50).

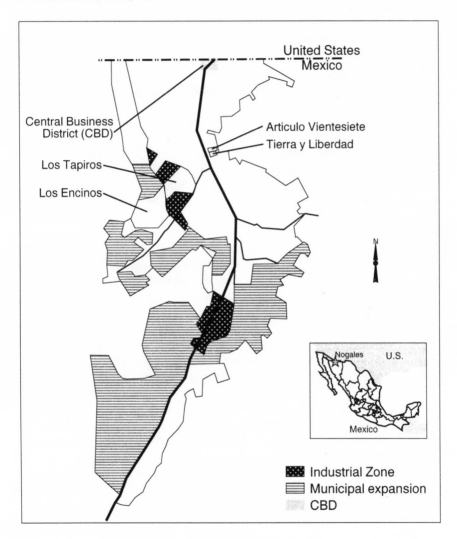

Figure 5.1 Nogales, Sonora

As the park's buildings were being constructed, Campbell leased space in downtown Nogales to small U.S. firms. However, when the park was near completion in 1970, the local economy was depressed. The prospect of fully equipped but empty buildings in his industrial park inspired Campbell. He began an aggressive campaign to attract prospective maquiladora owners and allay their fears of the uncertainties in the Mexican business environment. He assumed much of the risk for his clients by "supplying the labor force, building the warehouse space, negotiating with commerce officials in Mexico to handle the trade legalities, managing the companies' operations and handling their payroll" (*Arizona Daily Star* October 4, 1987). Campbell's role as an intermediate employer separated and therefore decreased state and corporate employers' responsibility for labor. The "shelter" plan, as Campbell's arrangement came to be called, refers to the fact that capital investments are sheltered. The shelter plan and its corporate worker dormitories became central to the evolution of the Nogales factory regime and the concomitant reorganization of social reproduction.

Shelter Plan

The shelter plan *(plan de albergue)* was first pioneered in the Nogales Industrial Park but has become a very common arrangement along the U.S.-Mexico border, contributing to the growth of the new factory regime (Sklair 1989, 48). The plan entails a special type of subcontracting arrangement that retains some of the advantages of direct production such as quality control and delivery specifications. A company entering into a shelter arrangement contracts with the U.S. arm of the shelter operator, which then contracts with its Mexican company. Clients are attracted to the plan because they can completely avoid legal involvement in Mexico. For a fee based on person-hours worked, the shelter operator assumes many of the risks. Richard Campbell implemented the arrangement with his partner from the industrial park development, Richard Bolin.

Samsonite and Memorex were among Campbell's first large U.S. clients to establish pilot operations under the shelter arrangement when the PINSA industrial park was finally inaugurated in late 1970. This event and other pivotal dates in recent Nogales history are noted in Table 5.1.

A corporation named Sonitronies-Collectron has continued to run the Nogales shelter plan through the 1980s and 1990s. Collectron Inc. of Arizona, the U.S. branch of the business, contracts with transnationals

Table 5.1 The Evolution of the Nogales Factory Regime

Date	Event
1965	Maquiladora program established
1967	Motorola opened
1970	Industrial park (PINSA) dedicated
1974-75	Industrywide crisis–U.S. recession
1980	AIRCO (now Jefel) strike
1981-82	2nd Industrywide crisis–recession
1981	12 factories sign CTM union agreement
1982	National crisis–Peso devaluation
1983	Maquiladora program extended to all of Mexico
1984	Dormitories established
1985	Los Tapiros land invasion
1987	Coleman union vote rejected (Nogales, Arizona)
1989	Los Encinos and Tierra y Libertad land invasions
1990	Artículo Veintesiete land invasion
1992	Jefel protests–collective grievance

Sources: *Arizona Daily Star,* November 1, 1967; June 30, 1970; June 9, 1985; March 4, 1987. *Nogales International,* December 26, 1974; April 10, 1975; May 22, 1982. Orantes, Lilia. 1987. Bietel, Tim. Manager, General Electric maquiladora, personal interview, February 6, 1992.

in order that Sonitronies S.A. (of Mexico) can contract with individual Mexican maquiladoras. In order to provide a flexible supply of labor to its client maquiladoras, Sonitronies operates worker dormitories as explained in the next chapter. More than twenty U.S. companies currently have shelter contracts with Collectron.

Labor Unrest and Union Activity

The history of labor struggle is at the core of this new factory regime's evolution. The maquiladora industry dominates the Nogales economy, employing more than half the local workforce. Since the late 1960s, when local industrialization began, periods of labor strife have corresponded to economic downturns that entailed work force reductions and high rates of unemployment. Although employers appear to exercise more power than in the past, workers have negotiated and resisted some aspects of their employment in the maquiladoras, especially during two recent periods of economic recession. In contrast to the previous model of industrialization, the state has withdrawn from active regulation of production. More important, the state has adapted its own corporatist structure to devise new means of labor control in support of the new factory regime.

During the brief history of labor unrest in Nogales maquiladoras, incidents and periods of worker activism have been followed by *increased* government concessions to business and by a strategy of labor control that utilizes the strongest official union in Mexico. There have been two periods of increased collective organizing activity and labor unrest. These periods were coextensive with economic downturns that included workforce reductions and high rates of unemployment. The first crisis period (1974 to 1975) was largely a result of recession in the United States that depressed the demand for electronic commodities. In Nogales, approximately 6,000 workers, or 31 percent of the local maquiladora workforce, were laid off at this time (*Nogales International* May 26, 1976; Carrillo and Hernandez 1985, 93; Orantes 1987, 57; Sklair 1989, 104). The second crisis period (1980 to 1982) resulted in more lay-offs, protest marches, several work stoppages, and a strike at AIRCO, a factory that supplies electric inductors to the U.S. military. The year 1982 marked a national crisis in Mexico, precipitated by falling oil prices and a debt burden that spun out of control.

The Crisis of 1974 to 1975

Seventeen factories, most of which were electronics assembly plants, closed during the 1974/75 crisis, while half of the remaining plants curtailed some operations and cut their workforce sharply (*Nogales International* April 17, 1975; Orantes 1987, 24). One of the more prominent maquiladora owners, computer component manufacturer Packard Bell, moved its local operation to Taiwan in September 1974 (Orantes 1987, 23). In March 1975, a unionization struggle erupted among 400 workers at the Señor Ricardo shirt factory (Irvine Industries in the United States), while 100 workers at the Bowmar calculator assembly plant staged a public protest after being laid off (*Nogales International* March 27, 1975). By April, problems at Bowmar had escalated to the point that workers, accompanied by workers from Micromex, an electronics firm, "stormed the state labor office in Hermosillo" 180 miles away demanding the reinstatement of their jobs (*Nogales International* April 10, 1975).

Most labor complaints during this time concerned the loss or possible loss of employment. In spite of legal guarantees and the permanent status of the employment relationship in Mexico historically, many of the 6,000 Nogales workers who lost their jobs were not compensated according to the law.

Government Response

The state responded to these unstable and difficult circumstances by granting further concessions to industry and by further relaxing enforcement of labor law. All maquiladoras were offered additional financial incentives and further remission of federal taxes. Within Sonora, the governor granted an extension of free zone status for five years (Ramírez 1988, 60). The free zone status streamlined importation procedures for the maquiladoras, which were permitted tariff-free importation of goods through the federal maquiladora program. The state also reduced the expense of social security payments that factory owners were required to pay. By federal law, the Instituto Mexicano de Seguro Social (IMSS) is required to classify all workplaces according to five levels of risk.[2] Employers are then assessed higher payments at higher-risk sites. To maintain high investment levels in Sonora, the state simply lowered the risk level evaluations for individual plants, thereby reducing the IMSS payments levied on maquiladoras (secretary of commerce, state of Sonora, cited in Orantes 1987, 25, note 19).

Other state efforts focused on promotion of the maquiladora industry. Acting in conjunction with the state of Arizona, city officials prepared and distributed a seventy-two-page promotional *International Community Prospectus* (1977) describing the local economy, labor market, and community services of Nogales. Female labor and the facilities of the modern industrial park were emphasized:

> The present available labor force of 9,000 reflects a current unemployment rate of 21.9 percent. Since the men in the active labor force out-number the women, the future labor pool can be increased through greater utilization of the female labor force. A state-sponsored labor survey in-

dicates that there are an additional 15,000 to 25,000 persons available within a 70-mile radius of Nogales. . . . The [industrial] park's paved roads curve through the slightly rolling terrain, and buildings are finished in Mexican motif. Every service and utility normally provided in U.S. parks is offered. Currently, more than 1,000,000 square feet of production and office area are contained in 23 buildings, and every structure is of concrete and steel beam construction. (56, 62)

At this time, the industry pushed for and won more control over the workforce through relaxation of federal labor law enforcement. The actions of Bowmar, one of the maquiladoras beset with labor protests, demonstrate the growing power of the employers in the new factory regime. In 1975 the factory closed and then reopened as a new company named IFR (Orantes 1987). Forming a new legal entity allowed Bowmar to rid themselves of activist employees who had been leading the protests, and at the same time facilitated the hiring of former employees, who had no seniority at IFR, at reduced wages.

This action by Bowmar was part of a comprehensive strategy in which the state cooperated with industry to stifle incipient union activity. Another effective part of the plan was the manipulation and repression of local labor grievances so that they would not be pursued at the regional or state level (Ramírez 1988). This involved Mexico's system of Conciliation and Arbitration Boards, which are the legal mediators of all labor disputes. Local grievances are heard by a board in Nogales. If unresolved there, disputes proceed to a Conciliation and Arbitration Board in the state capital city of Hermosillo, 180 miles away. In the aftermath of the 1970s recession, under intense pressure from the maquiladora owners and the U.S. Chamber of Commerce who threatened a corporate exodus, every effort was made to prevent grievances from advancing to Hermosillo. Workers were offered cash settlements, usually an amount that was much less than that requested. Those workers who did reach Hermosillo with a grievance faced a protracted hearing at great personal expense, a guaranteed adverse decision, and a probable black-listing in the Nogales maquiladoras (Ramírez 1988).

Problems in the Early 1980s

Employment levels recovered in 1978 and 1979, but low international demand and falling prices, particularly in the electronics sector, began to create new instability in Nogales maquiladoras in the early 1980s. Several smaller and medium-sized plants closed. For workers, months of insecurity over job tenure were followed by a steep overnight increase in the cost of living when, on February 18, 1982, the Mexican peso was devalued 45 percent. The impact was particularly acute for border residents because their cost of living is high and exchange rates have an immediate impact on the price of essential goods such as groceries. This hardship stimulated labor unrest, particularly work stoppages. The affected maquiladoras included Samsonite, a luggage manufacturer; Jeffers, an inductor producer; GE, an extension cord factory; Chamberlain, a garage-door-opener manufacturer; Molex, an electric switch and connector assembler; Deseret, a disposable medical device producer; Lowry, a cable assembler; Walbro, a carburetor plant; Señor Ricardo, a men's shirt factory; and Digital Development, an electronics enterprise (*Arizona Daily Star* April 13, 1982). Several months after the devaluation, the Mexican government suggested that maquiladoras grant a wage increase of up to 30 percent to offset the effect of the devaluation. The government encouraged this voluntary step by offering a reduction in the periodic factory licensing tax (*Nogales International* April 14, 1982). Although many firms granted the increase, it did not fully compensate for the devaluation. Overall employment levels were far more stable than in the previous period of crisis, as can be seen in Table 5.2.

The labor conflicts had unfortunate consequences for many workers. In May of 1982, the Señor Ricardo Company, having experienced labor unrest during both the early and recent crises, closed its factory and laid off the 186 remaining employees. In violation of the law, Señor Ricardo refused to pay severance pay to former employees. In other cases, workers were blacklisted for marching in protest of the peso devaluation, or fired for speaking to reporters or participating in work stoppages.

By far the most dramatic activity occurred at AIRCO, a company that also had severe problems during the 1974 crisis. In August of 1980, some 840 workers went on strike. The CTM, the most powerful union federation in Mexico, became involved but undermined the strength of the AIRCO workers. In this case, the local director of the CTM, Raúl Olmos, allied himself with the company and the strike eventually failed (Orantes 1987). Olmos has continued to be a local labor union leader and has also used his position to become an alderman in the City Council. After the strike had failed, AIRCO was closed and resurrected as Jefel in February of 1981. As in the Bowmar maneuver of 1975, the AIRCO action circum vented labor law by firing employees without just cause and without adequate compensation.

This type of contradictory behavior on the part of official unions is not unusual in the maquiladora industry (Carrillo V. 1991). As previ-

Table 5.2 Maquiladora Employment Levels in Nogales

Year	Number of Employees
1967	18
1968	535
1969	1,906
1970	3,014
1971	4,800
1972	5,800
1973	9,000
1974	9,827
1975	6,794
1976	7,078
1977	7,521
1978	8,849
1979	12,183
1980	12,921
1981	12,853
1982	12,363
1983	13,278
1984	15,964
1985	14,539
1986	15,252
1987	19,427
1988	22,864
1989	22,635

Although census data show a decline from 9,827 workers in 1974 to 6,794 in 1975, local newspapers and other sources report that 6,000 workers (31 percent of the local workforce) lost their jobs (*Nogales International* May 26, 1976; Carrillo V. and Hernandez, 1985, p. 93. Sklair 1989, p. 104; Orantes 1987, p. 57.

Sources: 1967-70 and 1972-74 entries from Orantes 1987, pp. 23 and 26. 1971 entry from *Arizona Daily Star*, September 12, 1971. 1975-83 entries from INEGI 1985. 1984-89 entries from INEGI 1990a.

ously discussed, the official unions have historically been organized at the national level and their leaders have been intimately linked with the PRI. A hierarchy of power within the official unions has often been used to manipulate local labor organization. In the far-flung spaces of the new factory regime, there is heightened concern that radicals will take over and challenge union hierarchy. Consumed with this fear, the CTM, the most powerful official labor federation in Mexico, *completely undermined* an attempt at collective bargaining in Nogales. This could *not* have happened in the older production sites or anywhere during the era of ISI happened in the older production sites or anywhere during the era of ISI growth. The labor union leaders who assumed powerful political positions in the ISI years achieved those positions by representing workers and articulating their collective demands. In this case, the CTM director chose to barter the confidence of the activist workers at the AIRCO plant for an improved position in local politics.

Nevertheless, labor unrest continued at the plant. In April of 1982, 100 workers marched in protest of work conditions. Their demands were for a wage increase, running water, drinking water, an end to mandatory overtime, and an end to supervised bathroom privileges.[3] These issues of basic human dignity and health would not have been contentious in the norms of the old factory regime. The early 1980s was a rocky period for the new regime. Plant closures plus sharp wage cuts created an uncertain environment for Nogales workers. Work stoppages were followed by protest marches and a large strike at the AIRCO/Jefel electronics plant. Although (or perhaps because) the official unions collaborated with the state to undermine the strike, the factory itself remained a local trouble spot through the mid-1990s.

"Company Union" Contracts

In February 1981, immediately following the AIRCO strike, fourteen of the largest factories in Nogales signed labor contracts with the CTM, the union which had worked to defeat collective bargaining at AIRCO.[4] These agreements are best understood as protection contracts with a company union, which protect maquiladora owners from other labor unions and from grass roots organizing. Local businessmen refer to the agreements as "desk drawer" contracts, because they can be filed away and forgotten. Some clauses contradict federal labor law by relaxing the conditions under which workers may be dismissed and by requiring mandatory overtime without pay. Most surprising of all, workers in these plants are unaware that they have a union, the CTM, representing them as well as a collective bargaining agreement pertaining to their workplace relationships (Orantes 1987; Denman 1988; Ramírez 1988).

The invisibility of the CTM in the Nogales maquiladoras demonstrates that the union is actively working to subvert worker organization and genuine collective bargaining. The election of the CTM leader Olmos to a prominent role in Nogales City Administration crystallized the local alliance of industry and the CTM. And the signing of CTM union contracts by a core group of large maquiladoras consolidated the new factory regime in Nogales. The triumvirate of industry, city government, and the official union guaranteed a stifling degree of control over local working conditions, and ushered in a period of *relative* stability. In spite of overwhelming odds against them, workers in Nogales have continued to resist. Grassroots organizing is a feature of daily life within squatter neighborhoods and on shopfloors. In 1991, maquiladora workers in one plant created an independent coalition in order to file a collective grievance against an employer–the first action of its kind in Nogales' history (Cravey 1993; 1998).

Labor conflict has not disappeared in Nogales. Two events in the last decade deserve examination. The first was a United Auto Workers (UAW) organizing drive among workers at a twin plant on the U.S. side of the line in Nogales, Arizona. Workers at the Coleman Products Company, a subsidiary of American Motors, staged a union election in order to improve their working conditions and wages, which ranged from $3.50 to $4.00 per hour. Local government officials, including the mayor, spoke publicly against the effort, stating that the company would move the factory across the line to Nogales or Ciudad Obregón, Sonora, if the union won the election. In spite of a *corporate* victory in the election, the plant subsequently relocated to Sonora (*Arizona Daily Star* March 1, 1987; March 4, 1987; July 9, 1988). During the same month, auto workers shut down a new half-billion-dollar Ford factory with a strike in Hermosillo, Sonora, several hours south of Nogales. The company responded with violence–kidnappings and beatings–in Hermosillo and in other factory locations (*Arizona Daily Star* March 2, 1987; March 12, 1987).

The Coleman UAW election and the Ford strike were local indications of a wave of increased political activity and union activism in Mexico in 1987. Electrical, telephone, university, and textile workers staged or attempted to stage national strikes. Meanwhile, several leftist parties allied with a dissident sector of the PRI, forming the Partido de la Revolución Democratica (PRD), the most powerful and unified opposition party known to modern Mexico.

The signing of CTM union contracts by a core group of large Nogales maquiladoras consolidated the new factory regime. A period of relative stability has been coordinated through a local alliance between industry, city officials, and the main official union. In the face of labor militancy, these actors have cooperated in order to maintain control over local working conditions.

Jefel de Mexico, an Isolated Pocket of Continuing Labor Strife

Jefel de Mexico, the maquiladora manufacturing inductors originally known as AIRCO, has had persistent labor problems. Problems in the factory surfaced in January 1991 when Vishay Technologies of Pennsylvania bought and merged Jefel with another Nogales maquiladora. The other factory, West-Cap of Arizona, a producer of capacitors and inductors, was closed and workers were transferred to Jefel (Leal, personal interview, November 11, 1991). Some of the workers were unhappy with the transition and the working conditions at Jefel, especially those who lost several years of seniority. They requested *licidación*, a formal termination. Licidación is guaranteed by Mexican labor law to workers when their employer has ceased production. Many companies try to avoid these payments.

The workers organized daily public demonstrations for four months, in an attempt to pressure the company for formal termination. Finally seven workers were fired, those who had been most active in organizing. Moreover, they were denied severance pay. Six of the workers filed a collective grievance at the local Conciliation and Arbitration Board on November 11, 1991, and were called for hearings in October 1992. Jefel de Mexico claimed that the workers forfeited their rights to severance pay by organizing daily public demonstrations for the four months preceding the firings. The workers responded that the protests had been external to the workplace, after hours, and completely legal.

This action set a precedent in Nogales, as the first collective grievance. Table 5.3 shows the annual number of labor demands from 1975 to 1992. In the case of Jefel, the group filing the complaint was not a union but a *coalición*, which was formed for the specific purpose of filing a grievance over an unfair labor practice.[5] In spite of persistent labor problems at Jefel, the new factory regime in Nogales and the local alliance that supports it remain stable.

The history of labor struggles in Nogales maquiladoras suggests that the state helped to undermine collective bargaining activity throughout the evolution of the new model of industrialization. In 1980, the unions themselves collaborated with the state to suppress the largest strike in Nogales history. Within six months, a core group of large maquiladoras signed (and certainly paid for) "protection" contracts with the official union federation to insure labor peace. The decentralized bargaining structures and decentralized regulatory structures of the new factory regime facilitated this contradictory behavior on the part of the unions. Union leaders acted in opposition to their membership in order to consolidate an alliance with local politicians

Table 5.3 Formal Demands Filed with the Junta de Conciliación

Year	Individual Demands	Collective Demands
1975	18	0
1976	6	0
1977	14	0
1978	5	0
1979	12	0
1980	20	0
1981	20	0
1982	40	0
1983	26	0
1984	22	0
1985	23	0
1986	9	0
1987	4	0
1988	15	0
1989	6	0
1990	3	0
1991	12	0
1992	6	1

Sources: Orantes 1987, p. 60. Franco, Concepción. Secretary, Junta de Conciliación, Nogales, personal interview, September 14, 1992.

and maintain their history of intimacy with the PRI. Whereas the state had aligned itself with the labor union movement during the ISI years so that labor enjoyed a superior position in the labor/capital relation, it now moved forcefully to tip the balance of power toward capital in the

Nogales factory regime. The realignment of labor union and state actors in this city reflected a broader realignment of social forces in northern Mexico that quickly spread throughout the entire country. In turn, the dynamic new growth and development strategy set in motion a new wave of labor resistance.

In a simultaneous and interconnected process, the state began to retrench on previous commitments to social provision. Along with a new organization of production, there is an ongoing reorganization of social reproduction, including such things as health care, housing, land for housing, meals during the working day, and child care.

Social Provision

In Ciudad Madero, the idea of a worker's right to housing, health care, and child care, was a fundamental and unquestioned part of the local factory regime. In the Nogales context these goods have been renegotiated and privatized and are no longer considered a right. This case study illustrates the profound changes that have occurred in the relationship between industrial workers, the state, and capital. Most striking of all, social provision has been partially commodified in the new factory regime. In the past, the state had aspired to provide complete medical care for industrial workers and their families. Housing, which had been somewhat de-commodified through the Instituto Nacional del Fondo de la Vivienda para los Trabajadores (INFONAVIT) program and other union-sponsored housing programs, has been completely re-commodified. The transition from the old to the new factory regime is complex, however, with the *employers* often providing some health care at the factory and, in some cases shelter as well, in the form of worker dormitories. Two of the largest factories are also providing child care.[6] These are perhaps the most complex changes. Goods that are necessary for survival (e.g., housing, child care, and health care) are in very limited supply, and in some cases available only through the employment relationship. This dependence tips the balance-of-power in the employee/employer relationship in favor of the employer.

The reorganization of social reproduction has profound gender consequences. Women assume many of the burdens of goods and services that have been commodified or partially commodified. That is, when the public clinic does not fully treat a child's illness, the child's mother may be the one who dedicates precious time to the period of convalescence. Similarly, when public housing is inadequate, women may devote considerable hours and days organizing squatters to invade property for makeshift homesites. Of course, when social goods become "private," men become involved in these activities as well. As we will see, complex negotiations over gender characterize the process.

The emerging factory regime in northern Mexico is the result of the interactions of three groups of actors: the state; transnational capitalists; and workers, families, and communities. Workers have struggled in an ad hoc fashion to meet their survival needs and, in the process, are affecting the trajectory of these changes. The most visible action has been the invasion of unused lands for the creation of neighborhoods. Families work together to apply pressure on authorities to get necessary infrastructure, or physically install systems themselves, as in the case of the squatter settlement Tierra Y Libertad. Against all odds, workers continue struggling to provide for themselves and asserting their right to earn an adequate living.

The state has helped to shape many of these changes. First the state devised the maquiladora program and subsequent renovations, which increasingly favored foreign industrial capital. The state also granted fiscal concessions and provided space and infrastructure for industrial developers. In addition, at the local, regional, and federal levels, the state coordinated and enforced a factory regime that is resistant to collective bargaining and the formation of unions. The reorientation of state expenditures included the allocation of infrastructural funds to finance industrial parks.

Transnational capitalists also have influenced these changes. Mobilizing pressure from U.S. organizations such as chambers of commerce, creating local business associations like the Nogales Maquiladora Association, and working within the Arizona-Sonora Commission and other governmental bodies, they have been effective at reshaping Mexican industrial policy in order to keep costs low and maximize profits.

State social policy is an integral part of both old and new factory regimes in Mexico. State policies with regard to social reproduction are the counterpart to production policies and are equally important to the overall model of capital accumulation. In the old factory regime, represented by Ciudad Madero, the state provision of benefits to industrial workers was made through two channels: direct provision from the state and provision through a state-owned industrial enterprise and its labor union. The result was that several necessary goods–health care, housing, child care, food, recreation–were completely or partly decommodified. In Nogales, many of these same goods are scarce and the channels of social access are different. As we will see, this reorientation has had gendered consequences. As state provision is scaled back, women in industrial sectors assume many additional burdens.

The reorganization of social reproduction reshapes relations between employee and employer. For Nogales workers, the national move from public to private provision resulted in increased vulnerability to local employers. In order to have access to many essential goods, workers need to maintain the employment relationship. National and regional reorganization thus affected workplace politics by reducing the bargaining power of workers. The following examines the reorganization of social reproduction in the Nogales factory regime in four areas: health care, child care, subsidized or free meals, and housing.

Health Care

There are three important channels of health care in Nogales: socialized health care within federal agencies; care provided by employers; and a system of private providers which includes private charitable institutions such as the Red Cross, "an important bottom line of health care provision" (Ward 1986, 111). Workers and their dependents are eligible for free health care at Clínica Hospital General de Zona #5 de IMSS, the local Social Security hospital serving Nogales and the nearby region. Mexican citizens who are not covered by IMSS, because they work in the informal economy or are unemployed, are eligible for treatment at the local office of the Secretaría de Salubridad y Asistencia, SSA.

A few maquiladoras provide medical care to close family members of their workers, while many of the larger maquiladoras in Nogales have a doctor or nurse on staff to provide medical care for employees. This latter practice, as the manager of a General Electric plant explained, "limits absenteeism for health reasons, and the company has fewer disabilities. It also saves travel and travel time to the social security office" (Bietel, personal interview, February 6, 1992). In addition, this practice can also save money for maquiladora owners. When a staff nurse or physician lowers the accident rate in a particular factory, the required monthly IMSS payments are reduced due to lower risk level categorization (Diaz Aguayo, personal interview, July 9, 1992). This process redistributes social costs throughout the larger health care system and transfers certain costs to individual households, women, and children. Paradoxically, while appearing beneficent in providing medical care on the shopfloor, these employers are imposing new social burdens on workers.

Factory health care is provided in addition to IMSS, but it undermines the system of socialized care in two ways. First, workers are encouraged not to report many work injuries to IMSS. This reduces the agency's ability to oversee and regulate the work environment and compromises their ability to compile accurate statistics on workplace hazards. Second, the relationship between the industry and the state has changed as the factories assume the burden of increased health care in the region (in large part due to the influx of migrants seeking factory work). This transfer of responsibility has enabled the local IMSS facility, although severely understaffed and ill-equipped, to maintain its operation on a severely constricted budget. Although the substitution of factory-based health care for socialized health care may be irrelevant from the point of view of either industry or the state, the transition is distressing for Nogales workers who encounter a less adequate health system and a less salubrious workplace. A few local examples of public health consequences and workplace consequences are elaborated below in the section on "Health Hazards."[7]

Child Care

Child care is provided to some Mexican workers through Social Security (IMSS), the same agency that provides health care. Employers throughout the country pay a total of 1 percent of all payroll into a special IMSS fund for this purpose. IMSS has one child care facility in Nogales, located in the industrial park. Currently caring for 214 children, its capacity is inadequate as it only covers the needs of eighty-one sets of parents. More than 300 parents are on the center's waiting list. Two of the larger maquiladoras, Chamberlain, an assembler of garage-door openers, and Wilson Jones, a paper products manufacturer, have attempted to compensate for inadequate public facilities by setting up child care centers within their factories. The Chamberlain center cares for ninety-six children while the Wilson Jones center cares for forty-eight, although both factories need a facility with greater capacity in order to meet the needs of their employees. In the mid-1990s, four other plants have been considering this option.

In a clear case of retrenchment on social provision, these private efforts are encouraged by the Mexican state. Rather than allocating IMSS money for more public buildings and increased staff, federal operating funds are made available to private factory owners who establish child care centers. To qualify, a company must first file a federal petition. Next, the maquiladora owner is required to submit to government inspection and underwrite the program in its initial stages. Petitions are subsequently reviewed and factories are inspected on a case-by-case basis. In the case of the Wilson Jones maquiladora, the company set up the child care center and paid the costs of the program for two years before it was approved for federal funds, which now cover 90 percent of the operating costs (Higgins, personal interview, March 19, 1992). This transfer of public responsibility for child care to private businesses underscores the dialectical connection between production and social reproduction within a given factory regime. When aspects of social reproduction like child care are reorganized, the norms and the politics of the employer/employee relationship are correspondingly changed.

The private provision of day care in Nogales by some of the large factories subtly undermines worker welfare. A few powerful employers provide the service, thus relieving some of the pressure on the state to expand the IMSS facility. But in the meantime, many Nogales workers do without a public benefit which was provided to industrial workers in the previous factory regime. Furthermore, as we will see in chapter seven, households in the new factory regime are more fluid and fragmented than industrial households of the past. With the loss of family support systems in northern Mexico, child care becomes increasingly burdensome. New networks of support must be devised for child care but someone bears the social costs. In Nogales, this burden often, but not exclusively, falls on women and other children. At any rate, the reorganization of child care responsibilities for industrial workers is a gendered process at both the micro-scale and the macro-scale.

Subsidized or Free Meals

Most of the large maquiladoras in Nogales provide either subsidized or free meals during working hours. Both Wilson Jones and Thermax workers receive free breakfast and lunch at the factory. Many workers express appreciation for this benefit. As Elena Zamora, an eighteen-year-old who has been working in a maquiladora for two years, stated: "I spend very little on food because I get breakfast and lunch at Thermax [the factory] every day. Sometimes, I buy a little thing for dinner" (Zamora, personal interview, May 2, 1992). Elena moved to Nogales from Hermosillo, Sonora, where the rest of her family still resides. For the two years that she has been away from home, she has lived in one of Sonitronies' dormitories.

In other factories such as Chamberlain and Avent, a subsidiary of Kimberly Clark that manufactures disposable hospital garb, 80 percent of the cost of lunch is subsidized by the owner, while workers pay the rest. Breakfast is not provided. For income tax purposes, these factory owners report this expenditure as a fringe benefit, rather than as pay-roll. This has the advantage of allowing owners to circumvent additional taxes, such as IMSS and INFONAVIT, which are calculated as a percentage of payroll. In any case, managers report that providing free or subsidized meals increases production while the cost to the corporation is almost inconsequential. Before these meals were institutionalized, many workers came to work hungry or malnourished (Fraser, personal interview, May 12, 1992). Once again, changes in the organization of social reproduction have become a fundamental part of local *production* norms. Workers who do not earn enough to eat a nutritious diet are sometimes provided with a high-energy meal at the beginning of their shift on the assembly line. Employers can keep wages at a subsistence level while supplying calories at strategic times during the working day.

Housing

A critical housing shortage has been obvious in Nogales for many years. It is here that the social costs of rapid industrialization and local population growth are most conspicuously revealed. Although the community had over 10,000 houses in 1975, a local PRI official reported that it needed approximately 6,400 more (*Arizona Daily Star* May 5, 1975). Nearly ten years later, the deficit in houses had grown to 11,000 or 12,000 units.[8]

Several initiatives have addressed the housing problem but none have been adequate. Two strategies, owner-built homes on invaded land and maquiladora dormitories, will be discussed below. Other approaches include: INFONAVIT federal housing projects which have completed 2,798 units; *Proyecto Esperanza*, a well-funded program run by the Nogales Maquiladora Association but which has only constructed one unit to date; and Habitat for Humanity, an international nonprofit group with religious affiliation, which has completed twelve units and has five under way. INFONAVIT announced in 1992 that instead of direct housing construction, it would extend loans to prospective homeowners. As of this federal redirection, public housing in Nogales is now completely commodified. This imposes a significant burden on industrial workers, many of whom arrive in Nogales or other border cities with little savings and minimal social support. Even with adequate personal resources, finding housing in a community that has a chronic deficit of housing units is challenging. One consequence of these various fluid housing arrangements is that people begin to think about family relationships being negotiable. And, of course, the transitory lifestyles that result have different implications for men and women. At any rate, some individuals and families end up in temporary sharing arrangements. Others find a regimented temporary alternative in former factory buildings that have been converted into corporate dormitories.

Dormitory. Single-sex worker dormitories are one example of unusual household forms that have emerged in the maquiladora factory regime. These highly regulated spaces provide a stark contrast with the chaotic squatter neighborhoods where many workers must establish their households. The dormitory system will be discussed in chapter 5.

Land Invasion. The invasion and settlement of unused land is a practice guaranteed by Article 27 of the Mexican Constitution but sometimes contested by local authorities. Groups of squatters have seized rural land throughout Mexico, and more recently, urban land as well. After an invasion occurs, local authorities sometimes evict unfortunate squatters by force. Groups that are well enough organized to resist eviction, but not strong enough to pose a threat, must begin a protracted legal process of "regularization" in order to obtain title and services for their homesites. In the most simple cases, squatters locate the absentee landowner and negotiate a selling price and terms for payment. When an agreement cannot be reached, city or state authorities may intervene and expropriate the land so it can be divided and sold.

Several land invasions in Nogales have provided land for squatter housing. In some cases the land has been sold to the squatters and some city services have been installed. In fact, much of the territory that now constitutes the city was first settled by recent migrants in this "informal" fashion. Pueblo Nuevo, a colonia or neighborhood that appears quite well established now, was once vacant land adjacent to the city dump. Squatters from the colonia protested regularly in front of city hall to obtain water and electric service. For some time, residents were unable to determine the identity of the landowner, but the city eventually provided them with city utilities anyway. Because these improvements vastly increased the value of the property, a landowner arrived to challenge the squatters (Weisman 1986). He was ultimately unsuccessful and the residents were able to obtain title.

Los Tápiros, a colonia named for its elder trees and home to approximately 600 families, has a different history. This large rocky property adjoins La Granja, an industrial area in which many of the residents work. The original group of about 430 families carefully planned and executed their takeover under cover of darkness in May of 1985 (Leal, personal interview, February 24, 1992; *Arizona Daily Star* January 19, 1986). They immediately erected make-shift housing from pieces of cardboard and plastic in order to reduce the possibility of eviction. During the first year, the squatters encountered many difficulties. The city made an effort to relocate the residents nearly one mile away, but the proposed site became unavailable when a land swap failed between Sonora and the federal government (*Arizona Daily Star* June 15, 1986). The neighboring landowner, who operates El Sin Fin (The Place Without End) junkyard, allegedly destroyed houses on the fringes of the settlement. Another source of trouble sprang from the ranks of the squatters themselves. Internal strife, aggravated by residents' allegiances to different political parties, created factions that refused to recognize the authority of elected leaders, and this has led to a disorganized colonia (*Arizona Daily Star* June 15, 1986).

Land invasions are a place-based community strategy that industrial workers use to compensate for their lack of access to necessary goods. Relying solely on their collective strength, workers fashion neighborhoods where there were none. While this represents an enormous social burden, the power of working together can also generate a sense of belonging and empowerment. These spaces of community organizing may well be potential sources of resistance to the new factory regime in the future. Compensatory methods that operate at a finer scale–an individual, household, or family scale–will be discussed in chapter 7. All are important indicators of the lower *quality* of jobs in the new factory regime.

Health Hazards: Work and Home Environment

No examination of the quality of maquiladora employment is complete without a discussion of the industry's attitude toward worker health. It is important to look at the hazards of the workplace itself and the more general public health risks associated with the growth of the industry. Studies have not addressed either of these questions comprehensively, but my research suggests that the risks are great. Hazards of the workplace include exposure to toxics as well as mutagenic and carcinogenic chemicals, the operation of dangerous and antiquated machinery that lacks safeguards to prevent injury, lack of protective equipment and clothing, stress or disease caused by long hours and repetitive motion, and a denial of information on chemicals in the workplace. Community-level risks include chemical exposure due to improper disposal of industry chemicals, lack of hygienic water delivery, storage and drainage in squatter communities, housing vulnerability to flood damage, and transportation accidents in an overcrowded city

(Carrillo and Jasis 1983; Arenal 1986; Denman 1988; Kochan 1989; Sánchez 1990b). The risks may actually be greater than these studies indicate because gaining access to information is frequently an obstacle for researchers pursuing this line of inquiry.

The deleterious impact of maquiladora employment on women workers in the Nogales area was documented by Catalina Denman of El Colegio de Sonora. She studied the birth weights of workers' children, a measure widely accepted as an excellent indicator of the health of the mother. Using a sample of 300 pregnant women workers, Denman concluded that chemical exposures and physical demands made on the women seriously debilitated them leading to a 14 percent incidence of low-birth-weight babies. Strikingly, this rate was three times that of the control group, pregnant women who worked in service occupations in Nogales (Denman 1988).

Because of the importance of the industry to the local and national economy, health issues related to the maquiladora industry become political issues in the Nogales context. Even those charged with enforcing health standards are affected by this politicized climate. Dr. Diaz Aguayo, a specialist in occupational health at IMSS, closed Prestolight maquiladora, a manufacturer of cable harnesses, in March of 1992. He had determined that forty-two workers in the factory had elevated levels of lead, a serious and cumulative poison, in their blood. He ordered the company to install adequate ventilation and provide respirators to workers in the plant. In addition, he was concerned about possible harm to children in an elementary school adjacent to the factory (Diaz Aguayo, personal interview, July 9, 1992). One week after Aguayo closed the factory, a separate government agency, the Centro de Salud asserted a claim of jurisdiction on the matter and allowed the plant to reopen without making any changes in the labor process. Diaz Aguayo did not object because he believed that an interagency struggle would have been futile and that he would have found no support for such a struggle among his colleagues at IMSS.

Long hours in the factories are a less dramatic but real threat to worker health. Maquiladoras commonly extend the working day beyond the limit of eight hours mandated by Mexican labor law. In addition, many workers complain that they are not allowed to take breaks for urination at reasonable frequencies during the day. A new local norm has been established through the collaboration of factory owners within the Nogales Maquiladora Association. This norm has gone unquestioned by both authorities and workers. In Nogales the working day in the factories is commonly ten hours and thirty minutes long, spawning a 52.5 hour work week (Denman 1988, 58).

The salient community health hazard associated with the new factory regime is the contamination of the underground water supply and further risk due to inadequate delivery and storage systems in the squatter communities. Analyses of water samples from a central well, El Tomatero, showed high levels of several industrial chemicals used in local factories including trihalomethanes (THMs) and volatile organic compounds (VOCs) (Kamp February 5, 1992; Laituri, August 12, 1992). Water from this well is piped to several neighborhoods in the central part of the city and is also delivered by truck to squatter communities that have not been connected to the water system. In these communities, the methods of water storage create considerable risk of additional contamination. Most residents store their water in fifty-five-gallon drums that have been discarded or sold by the factories. Frequently the drums were used previously to store chemicals. Some of the drums in use still bear warning labels (in English) that dangerous chemical residues make them unsafe for water storage. Thus many workers and their families are exposed to carcinogenic and teratogenic substances in their homes if not in their workplaces.

The dormitory and squatter residents face different sets of health hazards in their home environments. The former live in a totally regulated situation; the latter live in nearly unregulated communities. Although the dormitory residents generally have more hygienic living conditions, they encounter sexual abuse and psychological disturbances along with a loss of privacy and autonomy. Both groups face a range of serious problems, which are reflected in the high levels of low-birthweight babies born to women working in Nogales maquiladoras.

Notes

Portions of this chapter are reprinted with permission. See Cravey, Altha J., "Cowboys and Dinosaurs: Mexican Labor Unionism and the State, in Andrew Herod (ed.) *Organizing the Landscape: Labor Unionism in Geographical Perspective*. Minneapolis: University of Minnesota Press. 1998.

1. During the U.S. Civil War this area became the Territory of Arizona in 1863, and a state in 1912.

2. This is mandated by Article 78 and 79 of the Social Security Law, Ley del Seguro Social y Su Reglamiento. Dr. Diaz Aguayo reports that this remains standard practice in 1992. He notes that Nogales factories are required to send yearly reports to Hermosillo that substantiate risk levels. According to Diaz Aguayo, only eight of seventy-five Nogales factories are currently in compliance and thus have been paying much lower IMSS rates than those required by federal law.

3. See *Void Where Prohibited* (Linder 1998). Workplace regulation of bathroom activities is an increasingly common practice that can have debilitating health effects.

4. The companies and their products were Avent (disposable medical products), Jefel (inductors), Samson (luggage), Permamex (garage door openers and security systems), Tecnología Mexicana (ceramic capacitors), Charles E. Guillman (wire harnesses), Cambion Mexicana (capacitors), Metro-Mex de Nogales, Rockwell Collins (microwave and lightwave transmitters and receptors), Foster Grant (sunglasses), Micro-Mex (electronic assemblers), Badger Meter (fluid meters), D.P.I. de México (disposable medical goods), and Sonitronies (shelter operator). The union is El Sindicato Industrial Progresista de Trabajadores de Empresas Maquiladoras del Area de Nogales Sonora de la CTM.

5. According to Mexican labor law, a coalición may be formed for a limited and specific one-time purpose.

6. In the Mexican context, corporate provision of childcare is helpful to individual workers but in a larger sense undermines the national program of socialized care. Unlike the U.S. context, where on site day care might be viewed as enlightened, we must consider the impact of corporate child care on the national socialized system of the previous factory regime.

7. See Public Citizen report for an introduction to some of the literature on this topic.

8. A 1986 estimate of 11,000 was reported in *El Imparcial*, cited in Orantes 1987, p. 53, while a 1984 SEDUE estimate, cited in Ramirez 1988, p. 81, suggested the shortage was 11, 625.

6

Single-Sex Worker Dormitories

> The U.S.-Mexican border *es una herida abierta* where the Third
> World grates against the first and bleeds. And before a scab
> forms it hemorrhages again, the lifeblood of two worlds merging
> to form a third country–a border culture. Borders are set up to
> define the places that are safe and unsafe, to distinguish *us* from
> *them*. (Gloria Anzaldúa 1987. *Borderlands: La Frontera*, p. 3.)

The example of the transnational corporate dormitory is particularly
revealing because workplace, household, and community relationships
collapse onto one geographical site. Nogales maquiladora owners devised a solution to the local housing shortage that is reminiscent of
nineteenth-century U.S. industrialization in Lowell, Massachusetts. As
in Lowell, factory owners established single-sex dormitories in which
workers could pay a weekly fee in exchange for shelter. Thus, for the
period of dormitory residence, young workers in Nogales accept the imposition of factory discipline *at home* and at work. The smallest details of life are regulated. One consequence of this arrangement is the
individualization of the routines of daily life. Rules and rewards are
imposed on individuals alone. Failure to comply with this system of total discipline results in expulsion from the dormitory and from employment. For these workers, the maquiladora factory regime expands
to encompass "private" household relationships.

What happens when our private lives become suffused with corporate influence in the way they do for these workers? How does this
change the way we think about families? How does it change the relationships between parents and children? How does it change courtship,
marriage, and other relationships between men and women? How does

this corporate influence affect identity formation? How does it shape the meaning associated with gender? These are just a few of the questions that arise in this context.

For the most part, the individuals who reside in the dormitories are teenagers from interior rural areas. Many of them end up in Nogales after signing a contract with labor recruiters. Sixteen-year-old Ramón Delgado's experience is typical: "I heard about the jobs on a radio program in Carranza (his hometown). I thought I should give this a try and see if I could make more money than I make in the fields. My cousin and I signed up and got a ride to Nogales on a private bus" (Delgado, personal interview, May 3, 1992). When I talked with him, Ramón and his cousin had spent one weekend night in Sonitronies male dorm but did not yet know which factory they would be working in or how much they would be paid. They were both quite optimistic about the possibilities of personal advancement in Nogales.

The dormitory system in this city allows for greater corporate flexibility and profitability. How does worker housing do so? Workers could be recruited and brought to a central place of temporary housing when the labor demands were high, either as the result of new clients or an upturn in economic conditions. On the other hand, workers could be sent on their way when labor demand was slack or when they resisted the twenty-four-hour discipline of the dormitory. These cycles, in fact, have served to reinforce the intimate discipline of the dormitories because workers know that others will be recruited to take their place if they violate curfews or "misbehave" in other ways.

The dormitory system was also integral to the success of the original Nogales shelter plan *(plan de albergue)*, a method of sheltering capital investments that has been adapted for many other sites along the U.S. border. The shelter plan has a number of advantages for transnational capitalists, as we began to see in the last chapter. Most important, the shelter operator assumes much of the risk of his clients by taking care of all the details of daily operations from warehouse construction to labor supply. As an intermediate employer, the shelter operator separates and therefore decreases *both* the state and the corporate employers' responsibilities to workers at a particular worksite.

The dormitory system was crucial to the original shelter plan because labor supply was the most unpredictable part of the contractual arrangement. Transnational employers who were nervous about operating in Mexico were anxious, above all else, about the political stability of the local labor supply. Would workers maintain good productivity levels and good attendance records at current wage rates? Would they steer clear of unions and refrain from collective work actions? Would they be more easily controlled than their counterparts in Asian assembly zones? Shelter corporations were able to dispel these salient concerns of foreign investors, and, in doing so, were able to shape the maquiladora factory regime.

Nogales and its dormitories in one sense are not typical of the northern production region. That is, although the shelter plan has been implemented elsewhere, the dormitory has not been. What then can the dormitory system tell us about the maquiladora factory regime? As I explain in the appendix, I have chosen cases for comparison in order to draw the comparison at its most extreme. Elements of the maquiladora factory regime were created in the cocooned and controlled context of Nogales that might not have emerged elsewhere. By looking closely at these features–particularly the dormitory system–we can see the trajectory of the overall changes. In particular, we can see the ways in which social reproduction has been individualized, leading to the fragmentation of the social fabric. We can also see the most extreme effects of state welfare retrenchment. The cuts in public social programs were relatively more onerous for dormitory residents because the dormitory arrangement was a result of acute worker vulnerability during the U.S. recession of the mid-1970s. In these temporary "households," significantly more control is exerted over the lives of industrial workers through specification and control of activities after working hours. The arrangement reduces industry's cost of workforce reproduction, because the individual is being sustained, rather than the entire family.

What are the new labor practices of northern Mexico? And how uniform are they in this huge region of dispersed industrial development? Although there are some intriguing variations within the region, the pattern is surprisingly consistent. The homogeneity of the new factory regime is reinforced by competitive global processes whose short-term trends are closely watched by even the largest transnational employers. The norms of the new factory regime entail the reorganization of the labor process and the larger regulatory environment, changes that have been overwhelmingly disadvantageous to labor.

Corporate worker housing reflects this process of state retrenchment while ensuring flexibility for corporate managers in Nogales. A rather small proportion of Nogales' industrial workforce has resided in corporate dormitories at any point in time. In 1992 there were approximately 1,200 workers or 5.3 percent of the total workforce living in six large buildings owned by Sonitronies in the city. Estimates suggest that there might have been twice this many dormitory residents at various times in the past. These small numbers conceal the significance of the housing arrangement to the overall production system in the city. This available, and willingly temporary, labor pool is the element that allows the shelter plan operators to attract new foreign investment to Nogales. The workers involved have not made the same effort to secure land that many industrial workers have done. They can more easily return to a previous, perhaps agricultural, way of life, during a period of economic contraction in Nogales. The temporary nature of this labor pool then, is also the element that allows Nogales employers, through the coordination of the Nogales Maquiladora Association, to quickly increase or decrease labor supply to meet the needs of the prevailing trends.

Origins

The worker dormitories in Nogales are concealed by a pervasive pro-growth, pro-maquiladora attitude in the city. Due to the sensitive nature of this topic, even worker advocates that I spoke with were initially quite reluctant to discuss the dormitories or to reveal their locations. Perhaps these advocates feared that outsiders would sensationalize the realities of life in Nogales's corporate dormitories. The system originated during a difficult set of local circumstances. An innovative subcontracting arrangement led to the need for a centralized yet flexible labor supply. The Nogales shelter arrangement, as it is called, dates from the recessionary period of the early 1970s and the completion, by a local businessperson, of a large industrial park. Labor strife and the economic downturn threatened the businessperson's anticipated profits. Turning adversity to his advantage, however, he set up a subcontracting arrangement that, by assuming many of his clients' risks of doing business in Mexico, attracted a number of blue-chip investors. This shelter arrangement required a flexible labor supply for each client factory. After a number of years in operation, local shelter operators decided that company-owned worker housing would be the most efficient way to maintain this flexibility. Thus, in 1984, the largest shelter operator, Collectron/Sonitronies set up two extensive single-sex dormitories in vacant factory buildings. Ironically, one of these dormitories, Sonitronies Dormitorio Número Tres, is the same building at 554 Calle Obregón that originally housed Motorola, Nogales's first maquiladora (*Arizona Daily Star* 1967).

For 11,000 pesos or nearly 8 percent of their paycheck (about 3.70 U.S. dollars) weekly, workers receive a bed, a small locker identical to those commonly used in elementary schools in the United States, and access to a small kitchen, bathroom, laundry sink, and television.[1]

Workers have very little personal space within the buildings as rooms typically are completely filled with bunk beds that are pushed together in pairs so that only narrow passages remain. Each bunk is identified with a large printed number, and in some cases as many as forty-eight workers share a single room. Although most dormitory residents endure these crowded conditions by considering them a temporary inconvenience, some individuals do not adjust easily and seek out other arrangements. In this way they resist the twenty-four-hour regulation of their lives that the corporate dormitory represents. One worker, Maria Elena Sáenz, confided that she had used the excuse of a family visit in Guasave, Sinaloa, to quit her job and leave the crowded dormitory near a centrally located grocery store named VH. Upon her return a few weeks later, she found a job with Wilson Jones, a paper goods manufacturer that maintains smaller dormitories for some of its workers. Maria Elena said she was "much happier in this dormitory because there are only six people in my bedroom" (Sáenz, personal interview, March 28, 1992).

Gendered Identities

How are new gender identities being shaped in the dormitory? First and foremost, they are shaped by the daily interactions of large numbers of young people. A youth culture of hopeful enthusiasm, high energy, and the exploration of urban entertainment is apparent. A number of young women spoke about the pleasures of shopping on their day off work. One of the men, Raúl Hurtado, took satisfaction from playing soccer with his company team during his leisure time. When I asked if he enjoyed seeing the same people on Sunday that he sees during the week, he responded enthusiastically that "it's great to relax and drink and play with the guys during our free time" (Hurtado, personal interview, May 23, 1992). Whatever the daily routine may be, it takes place under highly regulated circumstances in the corporate dormitories. Company guards monitor the activities of residents at all times and enforce an evening curfew and strict lights-out policy. Discipline is imposed through a system of reprimands. A worker with three reprimands, for such offenses as coming in late or not reporting a destination when leaving the building, is subject to being expelled from the dormitory.[2] If this happens, a worker cannot return. Dormitory discipline is extended to every aspect of social reproduction including biological reproduction: pregnancy automatically results in expulsion (Monroy Aguilar, personal interview, March 28, 1992; Sáenz, personal interview, March 28, 1992).

These company regulations entail a loss of personal control, privacy, and security that, in turn, creates a host of problems. Isabel Guerrero of Centro Contra la Violencia reports that violence, psychological disturbance, and sexual abuse are common (Guerrero, personal interview, March 6, 1992). Theft is also prevalent (Carrasco, personal interview, January 14, 1992). According to local psychologists these effects combine to create a collective neurosis. Many residents offer little overt resistance to the highly regulated conditions of the dormitories. Some are surprisingly unaware of the restrictions imposed by the guards. One twenty-two-year-old woman, for example, invited me to accompany her from the street outside into the lobby of the dormitory after she had agreed to be interviewed. Even though I explained that I had been refused access to the dorms, she insisted that it would not be a problem for her to have a guest. We went inside, sat down near the entrance, and talked for perhaps two minutes before the guard came over and asked me to leave. To avoid an escalation of the incident, I explained to the guard that the misunderstanding was all my fault, apologized to the young woman, and exited from the building. The depth of this young woman's shock and embarrassment caused me to realize just how unaware she had been of certain constraints on her daily life in the dorms.

Identity formation for dormitory residents thus takes place under highly unusual circumstances. Each person is temporarily removed from a familial structure whose authority is replaced by a paternalistic transnational employer. Through a strategic alliance with the Mexican state, these employers derive nearly absolute power. Individual identities of the workers are thus negotiated with the managers and other corporate representatives while living, interacting, and cooperating with a large group of similarly positioned young people. Class and gender identities are forged in this super-heated crucible. How is this environment gendered? In one sense, it is de-gendered. Whether male or female, each youth spends considerable time (leisure and work time) with other young residents. The paternalistic discipline that is imposed within the dormitory is similar for males and females. The company guards do play a role in cultivating gender norms through encouraging such leisure activities as team sports for males and beauty and fashion events for females. A youth-centered culture emerges within the precious leisure hours available to male and female dormitory residents.

The individualization of domestic labor within the dormitories has an immediate impact on residents' notions of masculinity and femininity because all individuals must provide domestic labor for themselves. Enrique Gutiérrez confided that he was learning how to cook during his stay in the dormitory and that "getting together with a couple other guys for meals is easier than fixing my own" (Gutiérrez, personal interview, May 17, 1992). On the other hand, some of the women in the dormitories who had been burdened with considerable domestic labor in previous family situations viewed the individualization of tasks in the dormitories as liberatory. Three female cousins who had come to Nogales from the fishing community of Guasave happily told me that "we work as a collective and only spend about an hour a day" on tasks such as laundry, cooking, cleaning (López, personal interview, May 10, 1992).

While these residents were able to maintain close family linkages, others suggest that they feel isolated and unhappy to be removed from the security of their families. Many of the workers I spoke with visit their families frequently, including those workers who live at considerable distance from Nogales. A majority of the workers I spoke to also sent financial support home. In most cases these remittances went to workers' parents, although one twenty-nine-year-old man said that he sent 100,000 pesos (most of his salary and approximately equivalent to $33) to Ciudad Obregon each week. His wife and three children relied on these funds and had no other source of income.

Flexible Labor Supply

The dormitory system is a profitable enterprise in its own right. The inherent flexibility of the system allows Sonitronies, the shelter operator, to supply labor to more than twenty factories, receiving a percentage of every hour worked in addition to rental payments made by workers. Collectron Incorporated of Arizona, the U.S. branch of the business, contracts with transnationals in order that Sonitronies S.A. (of Mexico) can contract with individual Mexican maquiladoras. In order to provide a flexible supply of labor to its client factories, Sonitronies, the Mexican arm of the corporation, operates worker dormitories. Collectron runs ads in prominent business journals, offering a "relocation to Mexico" consulting service and seminar. The company boasts that its clients will save up to $25,000 yearly per worker by moving to Mexico. They also trumpet the lack of "red tape" involved. In 1992, well-known U.S. companies that employed dormitory workers included: ITT Cannon, a division of ITT; Sumex, a subsidiary of Xerox; Becton Dickinson, a health products enterprise; Datamex, a data-entry operation; Marquest, a medical products manufacturer; and ARS, a coupon-sorting operation.

The number of dormitory residents fluctuates widely over time to meet the needs of the participating factories. To maintain a supply of labor, the shelter company recruits resident workers throughout Mexico through radio spots announcing when recruiters will be in the local area. A steady stream of newcomers thus replaces residents who move on to establish other domestic arrangements after an average length of occupancy of fifteen months. The flexibility of the dormitory system is beneficial to corporate managers who can adjust labor supply on a week-by-week basis to meet labor demand. Workers frequently mention that they find ways to take advantage of the impermanence of the arrangement as well. Workers spoke about choosing among dorms, switching locations, and leaving crowded squatter households to live in dorms. Because they pay rent on a weekly interval, workers seem to view the dormitory household as a temporary solution in their lives. This attitude helps to explain how they endure the crowded, impersonal, and regimented conditions without expressing more overt resistance.

In addition to Sonitronies, one other maquiladora owner maintains dormitories. Wilson Jones, a former client of Sonitronies' shelter plan, established two small dorms, one for women in 1988 and one for men in 1989, after terminating the company's contractual arrangement with Sonitronies. The company recognized that the housing shortage in Nogales was not improving and knew that several of their workers living in the Sonitronies' dormitory would lose their housing arrangement when the company became an independent enterprise in Mexico. For this reason, they decided to maintain the dormitory alternative for their workers by converting two large houses into dormitories but only as a "stop-gap measure." Manager Tom Higgins believes that dormitories are a short-term solution, and that business and government leaders must work together to provide adequate housing in the city (Higgins, personal interview, March 19, 1992). The Wilson Jones dormitories are much less crowded than the Sonitronies buildings. In the women's dorm the forty-four residents share a dining room, kitchen, and three bathrooms. Six to eight women are assigned to each bedroom, while fourteen or fifteen women use each small bathroom for hand laundering of clothing in addition to body hygiene.

Only one of the Nogales dormitories is close to the factories. This is significant because public transportation in the city is both inadequate and dangerous. Transport is thus not only a logistical problem for individual workers but a significant public health problem. According to Diaz Aguayo, of the local Social Security hospital, injury rates for the journey to work in Nogales are much higher than national averages and actually exceed injury rates within the factories. Thus most of the workers living in dorms who ride public buses encounter a hazardous situation before and after the formal working day. The only dorm residents who can consistently avoid this danger are the approximately 400 men who live in the Sonitronies dorm near the industrial park.

The Significance of Dormitories

The Nogales dormitory system has been crucial to the operation of the local maquiladora factory regime. This flexible housing arrangement has allowed local business leaders to maintain a tighter control on labor than at other production locations in northern Mexico. The dormitory system has also allowed transnational corporations to adjust the labor supply with little overt worker resistance. Thus more workers can be recruited for peak moments of local economic cycles and subsequently dismissed during recessionary periods. By accepting temporary status, dormitory workers give local employers more control over the entire labor force, dormitory residents and squatter residents alike. How does this happen? The position of the most vulnerable workers–the dormitory residents–impacts the general level of exploitation because their example demonstrates to all local workers that a seemingly endless pool of temporary labor from rural Mexico is available as a reserve army of labor. Workers are less inclined to challenge their employers when their own employment status is insecure, because they know that they can be easily replaced. Whether the issue is having adequate opportunity to relieve oneself in the restroom or having an adequate wage, Nogales industrial workers are cautious, and reasonably so, about confronting their bosses.

In this chapter, I have speculated a bit about the consequences of the corporate dormitory system for gender, family relationship, and identity formation. Much more could be said; however, I will summarize by saying that the dormitory system illustrates the worst aspects of the maquiladora factory regime. This twenty-four-hour system of complete regulation shows us how social costs (to capitalists) can be minimized while creating a temporary supply of labor that can be adjusted to fit economic cycles. For workers, the impact of the new corporate spaces may be more ambiguous. In this exploitative environment, collective identities are forged and youth culture may continue to flourish. It is hard to predict, but there certainly may be unintended consequences of this nascent worker consciousness in the near future. What elements of the Nogales case constitute a general picture of the maquiladora factory regimes that we can compare and contrast with the previous state-led factory regime?

Notes

1. The 1992 peso was subsequently revalued so that, in comtemporary terms, the 11,000 pesos mentioned here is equivalent to 11 new pesos.
2. The evening curfew is 9 pm, with the exception of Saturday, when many workers stay out late, and Sunday, when they must report by 5 pm.

7

Comparative Household Formation: Analysis of Change

"... capitalism presented patriarchy with different challenges in different parts of the country. The questions was in what ways the terms of male dominance would be reformulated within these changed conditions. Further, this process of accommodation between capitalism and patriarchy produced a different synthesis of the two in different places. It was a synthesis which was clearly visible in the nature of gender relations, and in the lives of women." (Linda McDowell and Doreen Massey 1984. "A Woman's Place," p. 128.)

The restructuring of the Mexican economy that transformed a state-led import-substitution industry into an export-oriented one dominated by transnationals, has been facilitated by a restructuring of gender relations both in the workplace and in the domestic sphere. The male employee of the previous model of accumulation has been supplanted in the new factory regime. In the new industrial cities and regions, it has been well documented that the overwhelming majority of waged workers are women (Fernández-Kelly 1983a; Carrillo and Hernández 1985; Sklair 1989). Even in Nogales, a city with a relatively less feminized workforce, the industrial labor pool is 66 percent female (Orantes 1987, 40).

The restructuring of gender relations in the household and private lives of workers has been less readily visible, but nonetheless vital to the transition. A rigid household form, predominantly nuclear in Ciudad Madero and other locations of state-led industry (Thompson 1992, 162), has become fluid and flexible. In Nogales, households are taking a variety of new forms and devise many strategies to gain sufficient income to reproduce themselves and reproduce labor power.

These variations in household form serve to subsidize and depress the wages of maquiladora workers through a variety of processes. In the simplest of these, multiple wages are pooled to meet reproductive needs. This occurs in households of the extended type and those in which nonrelated individuals form a household or are invited to join a consanguineous unit. The practice of land invasion and squatter settlement has a similar effect on the wage. Through collective effort to meet their housing needs, communities of workers who claim homesites in the *colonias populares* supply their own housing outside the formal market and at minimal cost. In addition to these factors, some Nogales workers have nonwage sources of income that also serve to depress wages.

This reformulation of the household unit, as well as the increased involvement of women in waged work, has had an impact on the division of domestic labor. Whereas men in Ciudad Madero relied almost exclusively on the labor of their wives to tend to their reproductive needs, these tasks are often renegotiated in Nogales. The most dramatic evidence of men's contribution to domestic labor is the use of a sequential scheduling strategy in which men are responsible for child care during part of the day *on a regular basis*. In other instances in Nogales, men help with cooking, laundry, or grocery shopping.

For some Nogales workers, company-run dormitories offer the solution to the local housing shortage. For them, the dormitory becomes a new household in which daily social reproduction is organized. The dormitories are an unusual new form of household in Mexico, in which productive and reproductive activities are organized by transnational corporations. The highly regulated environment results in a loss of personal privacy and control for these workers. This, in turn, weakens their capacity for collective bargaining.

The most complex change for industrial workers in Nogales has been their changing relationship to the Mexican state, exemplified by the changing channels of social provision. Many social goods, such as housing, health care, and child care, which were abundantly provided by the state in Ciudad Madero during the years of import substitution industrialization (ISI), are in scarce supply in the borderlands. More significantly, those goods that are available are often much more closely tied to the employment relationship. Maquiladora workers and their families are thus more vulnerable to losing access to these goods and are forced into a weaker position for collective bargaining and other forms of political activity.

Household Relations

Mexican industry was transformed in the 1970s from a dynamic post-Revolutionary period of ISI-oriented, state-led growth into a period of foreign investment for export production. This transition was a direct result of a change in the nature of the state and a corresponding shift in the state's productive strategies. The industrial transformation did not occur in a vacuum, however. The profound economic changes influenced, and were influenced by, Mexican social relations. One aspect of the larger social structure that has not been adequately examined in relation to this transition is gender relations.

An understanding of the dynamic of household and gender relations is crucial to an understanding of broader, larger-scale economic and social change. The composition and organization of households as well as the gender division of labor within them are dialectically influenced by changes in the form of capitalist production. Thus household and gender changes in Mexico provide an explanatory key to the industrial transition, e.g., from state-led to neoliberal strategies. Using gender analysis, we can understand more completely how the state was able to thoroughly transform its productive strategy. In addition, this type of investigation helps to explain why this particular transformation was able to extract more surplus labor and thus was so successful at attracting international productive capital. To begin this analysis the concept of the "household" must be examined more closely.

The ideology behind the concept of a natural, autonomous, universal domestic domain (i.e., household) was persuasively exposed by Olivia Harris in 1981 who insisted that deeply embedded naturalistic notions of the domestic domain are used to justify the subordination of women. Rather than dispose of household analysis, Harris suggested that we examine the facile assumptions behind the idea of the household as a separate sphere of nature governed by a natural economy. If we are to take Harris seriously, households must be analyzed more carefully in particular times and places and with attention to intra-household relationships, particularly gendered relations between men and women.

A common feminist historical argument that *does* highlight gender relations is the idea that the expansion of capitalist organization of production at the time of the Industrial Revolution removed productive activities from household proximity and control and, at the same time, led to the *nucleation* of the household and family. More recently this broad nucleation thesis has been challenged as flawed (Brydon and Chant 1989, Smith and Wallerstein 1992). Critics have argued that nuclear families existed in some European precapitalist social formations and that extended family households persist in many capitalist ones. The exceptional cases indicated by Chant, Smith, Wallerstein and others are insufficient to refute the nucleation thesis, revealing more about the uneven nature of capitalist development and the importance of context than about the effect of proletarianization on household form.

The household is a historically, contextually variable category that is distinct from, but often confused with, the family. Smith and Wallerstein define the household as the "entity responsible for our continuing reproduction needs (food, shelter, clothing), . . . [that] puts together a number of different kinds of "income" in order to provide for these reproduction needs" (Smith and Wallerstein 1992, 7). A more precise understanding of intrahousehold relationships is possible if we recognize *individuals* as the bearers of class position and the household as the site of multiple class relations (Fraad, Resnick and Wolff 1989; Deere 1990). In this way, class and subsumed class processes within the household can be examined. This type of nonessentialist class analysis is beginning to lay the basis for a concrete way to theorize the intersection of class and gender within households.

Although geographers have begun to do household level research, there has been a limited amount of attention to the households of the Third World (but see Christopherson 1983a; 1983b; Chant 1985a; 1985b; 1991; Chant and Ward 1987; Pryer 1987; Sage 1993) In a study of three urban labor markets in central Mexico, Chant has shown that household form is a strong determinant of women's labor force participation; women from extended families and women-headed domestic units are more likely to engage in waged work (Chant 1991). But what about causality in the opposite direction? What about the impact of economic change and the increased participation of women in waged work on household structure?

Mexican Industrial Transition

As the Ciudad Madero and Nogales case studies demonstrate, an array of state policies, beginning with the Border Industrialization Program (maquiladora) policy in 1965, eroded a comprehensive factory regime based on a male, unionized, fairly well paid, stable workforce. This strategy was predominant from 1930 and remained so until roughly

1976. However, the new policies, which were at first limited to a twelve-mile wide strip of land along the U.S. border, established a new production regime based on a feminized, less organized, low-paid workforce in *new cities and regions*, which undercut the profitability of the old model. Faced with a changing international political economy, the state began to dismantle the old regime and allowed the decline of established labor norms in the old industrial territories.

Industrial production had been concentrated in central urban areas during the years of the state-led factory regime, particularly the cities of Guadalajara, Mexico City, and Monterrey. These areas continue to be industrial centers. However, northern regions, particularly the U.S.-Mexico border area, have attracted more investment in the past few decades than the old industrial places and have become a prototype for a new model of accumulation that was supported and encouraged by a revised state strategy.

The two labor markets chosen for comparison represent the regions that have been defined by distinct factory regimes: Nogales, Sonora, for the current maquiladora regime and Ciudad Madero, Tamaulipas, for the previous state-led regime. Industry in Nogales is dominated by electronics and other component assembly operations. Ciudad Madero has a long history of petroleum production as well as small and medium manufacturing enterprises. Figure 1.2 shows the locations of both cities while industrial sites of the old and new factory regimes are shown in Figure 1.1.

How did the industrial restructuring and relocation of industry impact gender and households? This question can be broken into several parts. What is the gender division of waged work? What type of households do industrial workers in these cities form? How do they organize domestic labor? What is the gender division of domestic labor? Have social programs such as health care, child care, and public housing been altered such that the relationship between workers and the state has changed?

These questions begin to address one side of the dialectic. The other side is equally important. How did existing systems of gender hierarchy and the existing organization of households influence the trajectory of the industrial transformation?

Comparative Household Formation

Households in the two case study cities reveal the effects of deepening capitalist relations at different periods in time. A spatially concentrated and highly regulated old factory regime helped shape a nuclear family norm in Ciudad Madero. When new practices emerged in northern Mexico, fault lines were exposed in northern industrial households. Workers in the Nogales case, responding to the new factory regime, devised a wide variety of household forms.[1] Struggles within households reflect and contribute to the highly exploitative labor relations characterizing the northern region. Coping with lower wages, lower skill levels, and decreased social benefits, these workers refashion the most intimate aspects of their daily lives.

Preliminary comparison of basic characteristics of the three sample population groups immediately reveals differences between old and new factory regimes but little distinction between Nogales squatter residents and dormitory residents (Table 7.1).[2] Industrial transition produced a new factory regime with far lower wages and less secure jobs. Madero workers (Group 1) representing the old factory regime are distinct from the two Nogales groups representing the new regime. Not only are they better paid, but they are also older and have more education than their counterparts. Their mean education level is nearly three years more than the Nogales squatter residents. The old regime helped to structure fairly stable communities composed of nuclear households surviving on the wage and benefit package of a male head-of-household.

These generalizations are consistent with other research on industry in the north, particularly within the maquiladora sector. High turnover rates have been reported among factory workers in Juárez and Tijuana (Fernández-Kelly 1983b; Carrillo V. 1985). By one contemporary estimate, in Ciudad Juárez approximately 20 percent of the workforce turns over every month, although this rate drops to 15 percent during periods of economic recession (La Botz 1992, 165). Low pay and difficult working conditions contribute to high rates of turnover. The average length of a maquiladora job is only three years (Fernández-Kelly 1983a, 67). These tenuous employment relationships add a layer of difficulty to the fragmentation exerted by the new factory regime on households, leading workers in our Nogales sample to negotiate many different household arrangements over time. More knowledge about the daily lives of the three sample groups will help us to understand the contrasts among them. In particular, information on who is in the house-

Table 7.1 General Characteristics of the Three Groups of Workers

	Group 1: Madero	Group 2: Squatters (Nogales)	Group 3: Dorm (Nogales)
Number	20	20	20
Age	28.3	24.5	20.9
Salary per week			
(in pesos)	403,000	147,000	145,727
(in dollars)	134	49	49
Household size	4.7	5.3	6.7[*]
Job tenure	7.5 years	16 months	15 months
Education	10.2 years	7.5 years	8.3 years
Origin	local	various	region

This figure denotes the average size of the household with which the individual identifies him- or herself rather than the dormitory group, which fluctuates as high as 400 in one residence. In most cases then, this figure represents the family of origin, although it is sometimes the family of choice, i.e., spouse and children.

Source: Field notes.

hold as well as how the household is organized will highlight causal dynamics.

Household Composition

The household is the locus of daily and long-term social reproduction. Individuals and families struggle to create households in which they can meet their daily needs and the needs of the next generation. There is a sharp distinction between the old and new regime industrial households that may reflect the different contexts in which these individual and collective needs are met. Significant theoretical differences emerge when the household composition and organization of the three groups are considered. This section will examine differences in household composition before turning to the pivotal issue of the gender division of labor.

Evidence from the households in Madero (of the old factory regime) lends support to the nucleation thesis–that the deepening of capitalist relations in Mexico during the import substitution industrialization (ISI) years helped to create a nuclear family norm based on a single income. Industrial households such as those in Madero were predominantly nuclear and able to survive from day to day and from generation to generation on the wage of a solitary male head of household. An examination of the more recent Mexican transition to a new factory regime, however, suggests that those very pressures which produced nucleation are causing further fracturing of the industrial household structure in new deregulated northern industrial zones. Production in the new factory regime is far less protected from international competition than had been the case in the old regime. In the northern region, the effort by transnational employers to lower the cost of social reproduction relies on the expansion of the labor market to include younger female and male workers. These workers, in turn, find the wage insufficient for the nuclear family norm of industrial workers elsewhere and therefore develop other household forms. The evidence below suggests that the same forces of fragmentation that created a nuclear family norm now threaten to further atomize the social fabric.

The composition of three groups of worker households, sorted into five categories–nuclear, female-headed, extended, non-kin, and single-person households–is shown in Table 7.2.[3] Whereas the nuclear household is dominant in the Madero sample, reported by fifteen of the twenty workers, the extended household is prevalent in Nogales, described by nine of the twenty interviewees. The Madero nuclear households consistently rely on a male wage (a family wage) and a female partner whose work is centered on domestic tasks (a housewife). This holds true for different age groups. It is also consistent with informants' recollections of previous households.

It is worthwhile to note exceptions to the nuclear ideal in the Madero sample. Most of these had been nuclear households in the past and changed after the loss of the male breadwinner. For instance, two female-headed households in the sample included a widowed mother who lived with three teenage children and one single unmarried working mother living with her six-year-old daughter. The two extended households in the sample were quite similar in form. In both cases, a son had brought a young wife into the household for the early period of their marriage. In one, a twenty-year-old PEMEX worker emphasized

Table 7.2 Composition of Worker Households

Group 1: Madero	Group 2: Nogales
nuclear households: M*F*-3C M*F*-3C M*F*-3C M*F*-2C M*F*-2C M*F*-2C M*F*-4C M*F*-2C MF-2*C* MF-2*C* MF-12*C* MF-6*C* MF-4*C* M*F* M*F*	*M*F-3C *M*F-3C M*F*-1C M*F*-1C M*F*-1C MF-4*C* F-7*C*
female-headed (nuclear) households: *M*-1C M-3*C*	*M*-1C *M*-3C (1C working elsewhere)
extended households: MF-2*C*-1 wife M-3*C*-1 wife	*M*F-2C-2 grandparents M-M-*1 grandchild* M-5*C*-1 grandchild *Man*-dependent mother *M*F-5C-1 sister MF-2C-2 *brothers* M-MF-5*C*-1 brother-1 friend MF-2 sisters-1 *brother* M-4*C*-7 cousins
non-kin:	2 *female roommates*
singles: *1 male*	*1 male*

Key: M = mother, F = father, C = child, interviewee identified by underlined italic typeface. Source: field notes.

his desire to save money quickly in order to establish a home with his seventeen-year-old wife. In the second, the arrangement seemed less temporary because, as the respondent Luis Hinojosa explained, "My mother is a widow and enjoys having us all [himself, his sister, his brother, and his brother's wife] here in the house with her" (Hinojosa, personal interview, July 30, 1992). The house was quite large and comfortable for the five living there. In addition to these cases, one twenty-four-year-old man lived alone. No unrelated people lived in any of the Madero households and no more than two generations lived together in any household.

Households assume many different forms among Nogales squatter residents. The nuclear family characterizes less than half (seven) of the households in this sample. In addition, the sample includes two female-headed households: a young unmarried working mother with a baby and a thirty-year-old single mother of four. Ana, the thirty-year-old, provided for her children by working two jobs, a day job at a food stand and a night job at a factory. She also sent one of her sons (age ten) to live with her sister in another part of the city, where he works as a street vendor. During the period of the study, Ana decided to quit her job at the food stand and market her flour tortillas independently from her home.

Extended households are the predominant form in the new factory regime. Of the nine instances of extended households, four were extended vertically to another generation, while five were extended laterally to siblings, cousins, and friends. Respondents were quick to explain that expanding the household was often a conscious survival strategy. The more people in the household, the more labor was available for social reproductive and productive tasks. That is, additional individuals could contribute another paycheck or provide domestic services for employed members of the household. The vertically extended households in Nogales included a pair of working grandparents, a chronically ill grandmother, a baby of one of the unmarried daughters, and an openly homosexual man who cared for his mentally unstable sixty-eight-year-old mother.

The laterally extended households commonly expand to include the brother or sister of a married couple. In one case, the wife's sister (who was fourteen and still attending school) had moved to Nogales from Sinaloa to help with child care. Without the young sister's labor, the family explained, it would have been almost impossible to make ends meet. In another household, two brothers had moved from Veracruz with their sister's family, which consisted of her husband and children, so that all four adults could work in the factories. An atypical arrangement in the Los Encinos neighborhood included a working grandmother as well as a brother and his friend who moved from another state in order to work in Nogales. In one unique household, four siblings lived with the spouse of one of the four, all five working at maquiladoras; a second (male) spouse of one of the siblings had been left behind in Sinaloa to care for their two children while his wife worked in Nogales. In another extended household, a large family with four children shared a house with seven cousins; of the four children and seven cousins, three worked together in the same electronics assembly plant; most of the others were still in school. In another case, two unrelated women, one of whom was pregnant, lived together. Only one person in the sample lived alone–a single man, aged twenty-nine, from Baja California.

Nogales households assume multiple forms, with nuclear families existing alongside extended families and non-kin households. Group 3 respondents live in an institutionalized form of non-kin household, the company-run worker dormitory. Within these dormitory households, social reproduction is individualized, as well as temporally and spatially restricted. There is no social mechanism in the company-run dormitories for meeting long-term needs, so that each worker must determine for herself or himself how long to postpone (and how to provide for) her or his own future. Family connections are strained by employers' rules that workers must live individually, requiring workers to leave behind parents, siblings, spouses, and even children to rent one of the small numbered bunks crowded into former factory buildings. Although the dormitory itself becomes a new household for dorm residents, most see it as a temporary period in their lives and maintain strong attachments to families outside. Only one member of the dormitory sample was married. His family, consisting of his wife, daughter, and two adopted sons, live in Los Mochis, Sinaloa, and depend entirely on his income from the factory. All other residents in the sample are unmarried. Many send money home to their parents and siblings.

Gender Division of Domestic Labor

An analysis of household domestic labor provides an important contrast between the two factory regimes. Particular gender systems and specific models of capital accumulation reinforce each other. In the rigid nuclear household of the old factory regime, one woman typically did the domestic labor for the household. In the new factory regime, all aspects of daily social reproductive labor appear to be open to negotiation. As individual Nogales households adapt to change, such as fluctuations in income and household composition, household members devise new arrangements for meeting daily and long-term needs. Negotiations over the simple tasks of child care, cleaning, shopping, and cooking are less simple than they might seem at first glance. The result may challenge long-standing gender norms, amounting even to a renegotiation of the social meaning of gender itself. For instance, one male informant who regularly cares for his children during his wife's hours at the factory seemed to downplay his sustained domestic labor, as if it contradicted his ideal self-image. He and his partner had settled on this arrangement after a long period of fighting over the expense of paying a neighbor for child care. Negotiations may also be seen as class processes within the household, although they are not capitalist class processes. In the old factory regime, the household gender division of labor followed a predictable pattern: women labored within the household and men labored outside it. The man's wage (from outside employment) was considered a family wage, because it allowed the household to maintain itself over time. In this arrangement, women did more social reproductive labor than necessary for their own survival, and men benefited from this surplus. The new factory regime creates conditions of crisis in such household class relations. These have not been fully resolved and can be readily observed in ongoing negotiations in Nogales households. Tasks of daily social reproduction require significant amounts of time and effort because of a lack of modern conveniences. The absence of piped water, electricity, and adequate public transportation adds to the labor-intensive nature of mundane chores in new industrial regions.

There is a striking change in the organization of domestic labor during the contemporary industrial transition. In the new regime, males contribute significantly more labor to domestic tasks (Table 7.3). In 45 percent of all Madero households, one woman performs all the household reproductive tasks, and in 70 percent of all households these tasks are done by one or more women. By contrast, only 15 percent of Nogales households rely exclusively on the domestic labor of one woman, and 40 percent of these households accomplish domestic tasks with only female labor (one or more women cooperating). Therefore, although males contribute domestic labor in only 30 percent of Madero households, they are active in 60 percent of Nogales households. Similar gender relationships hold when only nuclear households are compared (Table 7.4). In this subset, males in nuclear households were more than twice as likely to contribute domestic reproductive labor in Nogales as in Madero. The differences are qualitative as well as quantitative. In Nogales it is common to find men who *regularly* assume responsibility for some domestic tasks. For instance, it is not uncommon for husbands and wives to alternate work schedules, one working the day shift, the

Table 7.3 Gender Division of Household Labor, All Households

labor done by:	Group 1: Madero	Group 2: Nogales
one female alone	45%	15%
one or more females	70%	40%
some adult male contribution	30%	60%

Source: Calculated from field notes.

Table 7.4 Gender Division of Household Labor, Nuclear Families

labor done by:	Group 1: Madero	Group 2: Nogales
one female alone	53%	29%
one or more females	66%	29%
some adult male contribution	33%	71%

Source: Calculated from field notes.

other the night shift, so they can share child care responsibilities. As Laura Ortiz Mora said about child care in her family, "My husband takes care of the children. He has to take care of them because I work [in the factory] at night. We take turns with it every day" (Ortiz Mora, personal interview, May 17, 1992).

Women's responsibility for child care has been thoroughly discussed in the literature as a nearly universal constraint on women's paid employment options (Mackintosh 1981; Folbre 1986; Momsen and Townsend 1987; Bowlby et al. 1989). One of several working-class strategies for overcoming this constraint in the First World is sequential scheduling, in which husbands and wives coordinate their work schedules so one can be at home with the children all day (Lamphere

1987; Pratt and Hanson 1991b). Sequential scheduling is significant, because as Pratt and Hanson (1991b, 69) comment, "the men in these households are taking sole responsibility for child-care for a portion of each day. . . . In other words, men are contributing a considerable amount of domestic labour . . . so that women can take employment outside the home."

This strategy has not been observed previously in Third World contexts. Of seven Nogales households with a husband, wife, and small children (under age thirteen), three couples deliberately coordinate their schedules to share child care. In two of these cases, the women work at night and take care of the children during the day. The strategy was reversed in the third case, where the man works at night and takes care of the children during the day.

In one of these households, a family with five children, ages nine, eight, seven, five, and two, the sequential scheduling strategy had been modified the month before my interview. The mother had been working the night shift at the Chamberlain maquiladora for nearly a year and previously had done the same for over two years at a now-defunct factory. She said that her husband had become overwhelmed with his domestic labor during the hours she was away. To help him with the children in the evenings, they invited her fourteen-year-old sister to move to Nogales from Sinaloa. The sister enrolled in school and assisted with domestic tasks as she integrated herself into her new household.

Male contributions to domestic labor in Madero were considerably less regular and sustained than in Nogales. Of the six households reporting some male contribution, two efforts were from husbands who occasionally help with child care and three were from husbands who sometimes help with cooking. None of these men said they made a consistent effort to relieve their wives. For example, when I questioned one father who takes care of his fourteen-month-old daughter, Antonio Fernández said, "My wife takes care of her during the day, but when I come home in the evening we share." When pressed about the help he provides, he said, "most of all I like to play with her and watch her while she plays" (Fernández, personal interview, July 30, 1992). Men help with the cooking in three Madero households and in seven Nogales households. In most cases it was stated that, "we both cook" or "we all cook together," making difficult an assessment of how much male assistance was contributed. However, none of these men in either sample had a regular commitment to cooking except a Nogales man whose mother was mentally ill and incapable of cooking.

Similarly, no men in either city regularly did all the household laundry tasks. In Madero, no men claimed to help with laundry. In three Nogales households men had some laundry responsibilities. In one home, the husband said he helps with the laundry. In another home, a man living with his sister's family explained: "I work at night so I do my own laundry. Once in a while I wash clothes for the rest of the family, but my sister usually takes care of it." In another household, composed of a widow, her four children, and their seven cousins, laundry was done by each individual, although cooking in the same household was collectivized.

For the dormitory residents (Group 3), domestic labor is individualized. Shelter and bedding are provided for a weekly fee, but each resident must prepare her own meals, wash her own laundry, and clean up after herself. Company guards, present at all times, may enforce order in the performance of domestic labor, but in no cases are they reported as assisting. Most dormitory residents therefore do all their own domestic labor. All interviewees from the large dorms run by Sonitronies report that they do their own laundry, cooking, shopping, and cleaning. However, in the smaller, more home-like dormitories owned by the Wilson Jones maquiladora, I observed several cases of spontaneous cooperation among residents for the organization of domestic labor. In these two dorms, one male, the other female, some residents used informal cooking collectives to prepare evening and weekend meals. According to Manuel Herrera, who had lived in the Wilson Jones dorm for three months, "It's easier to get together with one or two guys and prepare dinner" (Herrera, personal interview, May 10, 1992). Similarly, a group of three cousins from rural Sonora did all their grocery shopping and cooking as a unit in Wilson Jones's female dorm.

Household composition and organization are thus starkly contrasted in the two factory regimes. In Ciudad Madero, industrial workers prefer nuclear households that change very little over time. Even individuals from non-nuclear households of the old industrial regime tend to explain the composition of their own household by referring to the "ideal" of the nuclear household. Households in the new factory regime are more changeable and flexible. The household often becomes the arena in which Nogales workers strategize about daily and long-term survival needs. Unlike the households of the old factory regime, workers occasionally share a household with unrelated individuals and frequently share a household with more than two generations. Workers adapt the composition of the household to meet individual and collective needs. It may expand to include siblings, friends, or another generation. The arrangement may be temporary or long term, but respondents exhibit willingness to adjust to frequent change and embrace creative solutions that often involve a redefinition of the household. Literally, necessity is the mother of invention!

Within the diverse household forms of the new factory regime, it is clear that domestic labor has been drastically reorganized. For some workers, this change has been imposed by the discipline of the company dormitory and its twenty-four-hour guard system. Most domestic chores are individualized in the dorm, but workers sometimes form affinity groups to share everyday duties such as cooking. Squatter residents, on the other hand, devise patterns of domestic labor to fit changing circumstances. The outcome, I would suggest, has been the result of ongoing class and gender struggles inside (and outside) the household over surplus labor. To analyze these struggles, we need to see individuals as bearers of class position yet capable of participating in multiple class processes. For instance, the typical male industrial worker in Madero loses surplus labor to his employer, but gains surplus labor from his wife in the form of use values such as warm meals, clean clothes, and fresh produce. Since the family wage has been dismantled in the new factory regime, class and gender processes within households have become the locus of additional struggle and negotiation. The male worker mentioned at the beginning of this section who downplays his own substantial contribution to child care continues to struggle with himself over conventional notions of gender but, as a result of household negotiations, is actively creating new conventions by sharing the burden of domestic labor with his wife. His struggles and those of others like him result in the invention of new male (and female) identities. Thus the level and variety of male assistance with domestic tasks in Nogales, in stark contrast to the households of Ciudad Madero, result from micro-scale politics of reproduction. The sequential scheduling strategy represents a regular commitment of time and responsibility from males. In both nuclear and non-nuclear households, it is much less common to find one woman shouldering all daily domestic chores.

State Social Provision

A comparison of the two cities shows changing relationships between industrial workers and the state. This change is most visible in the uneven geography of public social programs. The old factory regime involved various types of social provision which lent stability to state/worker relations and, in turn, encouraged a particular gendering of capitalist production.[4] However, social policies are an integral part of old and new factory regimes in Mexico. State policies regarding social reproduction are the counterpart of policies toward production and are equally important to the overall model of capital accumulation. In Ciudad Madero, representing the old factory regime, the state provides benefits through two channels: direct provision from the state and provision through a state-owned industry and its labor union. Several categories of necessary goods (health care, housing, child care, food, and recreation) are decommodified or partly decommodified.

In Nogales, many of these goods are scarce, and the channels of social access are different. The regulatory role of the state, which had nurtured domestic industrial capitalists and industrial workers in the old factory regime, has been completely revamped in favor of transnational capital accumulation. Social policy complements industrial policy in providing transnational corporations (TNCs) with a dependent and quiescent workforce in the new industrial regions. How has this happened? Social funding has historically been geographically uneven, and pesos in the federal social budget were disproportionately allocated to central urban areas in the old factory regime. The retrenchment following the 1982 debt crisis exacerbated this regional imbalance. To avoid financial collapse by attracting more TNC investment, state actors scrambled to reinvent social policy and to construct new channels of social provision. A number of scholars are analyzing the details of these immensely complex changes in Mexican social policy (Cook, Middlebrook, and Molinar Horcasitas 1994; Cornelius, Craig, and Fox 1994). Suffice it to say that the general direction of change has been to dismantle, deregulate, and privatize social provision. Goods considered social *rights* in Ciudad Madero have become social *privileges* in Nogales. Some necessary goods were recommodified or became available only through the employment relationship. In the new production sites, the state has emerged as a powerful ally of the employer by dismantling traditional networks of social provision, thus making workers more dependent on their employers.

All the Madero workers interviewed had state health insurance; the fourteen PEMEX workers have company health plans and the others have federal health care provided through the Instituto Mexicano de Seguro Social (IMSS), a comprehensive federal health care provider funded through employer and employee contributions. All are satisfied with their access to medical care. Federally funded child care is abundantly available through these two agencies. Only four workers in the sample rent a house. The rest either own their houses or are in the process of buying them. Eight of the workers had benefited from a state housing program, two through INFONAVIT (the federal program for general workers) and six through a PEMEX program. Such public social programs helped create and sustain the old factory regime as well as a particular form of gender relations in nuclear households. The federal guarantee of comprehensive health care to workers and their dependents was most important in this regard. From the early 1940s, IMSS established a community and regional standard in central Mexico that helped to stabilize employee/employer relations during the ISI years. The family wage supporting the old factory regime was subsidized by a public benefit package designed around the male worker providing for a nuclear family.

What has been the experience of industrial workers in the north with these federal programs? All Nogales squatter residents in the sample are insured through IMSS and many report they have access to a doctor or nurse at the factory as well. In spite of having free benefits at IMSS, many visit private doctors because they cannot afford the time needed to see an IMSS doctor (in northern clinics that are understaffed and underfunded). The sentiment of a twenty-nine-year-old man from Veracruz, Juan Alfaro Zavalo, is typical: "We never go to Social Security (IMSS). We can't afford to wait all day to see the doctor" (Alfaro Zavala, personal interview, May 23, 1992). There are mixed opinions about factory doctors. Some feel that the company doctor is only capable of handling minor problems, others that the doctor is useful only for emergencies, some have no experience with the company doctor, and still others consider the service beneficial. One example demonstrates that social provision is now more tightly bound to the employment relation. A single mother who works at Avent (a health products factory) described an accident in which her young daughter, a U.S. citizen born in California, needed emergency treatment, "Ismelda was hurt at school and her ear was bleeding badly. She couldn't go to Social Security [IMSS] because she was born in the U.S. I ran to see the nurse [at the Avent maquiladora] and she called a private doctor who treated her for free (Hernández Navarette, personal interview, March 30, 1992)." This mother's good record of employment at the factory enabled her to secure the medical care her daughter needed. Even though help was unavailable from the state, her long and close relationship with her employer guaranteed the necessary treatment. All dormitory residents have access to medical care through IMSS. Many also are aware that they can see a company doctor at their workplace if needed, although few consult one. Several dormitory workers state that they are never sick, so they do not need a doctor.

Unlike the workers in Ciudad Madero, few Nogales workers have access to federally funded child care. Although employers in both cities pay into a 5 percent child care fund, the IMSS facilities in Nogales are inadequate and understaffed. None of the individuals in the sample has been able to enroll a child in the IMSS child care center, although some have been on a waiting list for several years. By the same token, few Nogales workers have access to state housing programs. None of the sample has received public housing. However, factory managers sometimes benefit from public housing in the new industrial regime. Workers and employers in the new northern industrial regions complain that they pay large sums to support federal housing and child care funds that spend most of their funds in the old industrial regions.

Private provision of health care and child care, along with changes in the administration of public housing, has undermined the system of public social services in Nogales. Fewer of these public goods have been made available to workers in the borderlands. For instance, the Nogales IMSS has fewer hospitals, doctors, and funds per capita than that agency in Ciudad Madero. The same can be said for public housing and child care funds and facilities. There is a *qualitative* difference in services provided. In a variety of ways, social services have become more tightly bound to the employment relation. This makes workers far more vulnerable to the whims of their employers and renders access to social goods more insecure, especially given the high turnover rates and short average tenure of maquiladora employment. In turn, such changes weaken workers' positions when bargaining over conditions of employment. The geographically uneven nature of social provision reinforces differences in the development of the two industrial regions.

Household Economies

Household income sources and spending provides a final point of contrast among the three groups of workers. Madero workers are the most fully proletarianized of the three groups and spend slightly less of their total wage on essential food and housing. Table 7.5 includes a summary of wage allocation for the three groups of workers. Madero workers and Nogales squatter residents spend nearly the same percentage of their wages on food and housing. However, because squatters pay little or nothing for irregular housing, this entire portion (which typically includes several wages) is allocated to the food budget. For dormitory residents, the 32 percent of the wage earmarked for necessities is much lower, reflecting the individualized nature of social reproduction

Table 7.5 Income Allocations and Sources

	Group 1: Madero	Group 2: Squatters Nogales	Group 3: Dorm Nogales
Income allocated for essentials:			
% income on food	42	59	24
% income on housing	14	0[a]	8
Total	56	59	32
Nonwage sources	0	5	4

a. One respondent did report that she had just begun paying 200,000 pesos per month to INDEUR, a Sonoran government agency, for payment on her lot. She said she would have the property paid in full in five years (Serrano, personal interview, March 16, 1992).

Source: Calculated from field notes.

for this group. In contrast to the others, many dormitory residents send a portion of their earnings to their families in another location, helping thereby to sustain social reproduction separated in space.

Both groups of Nogales residents occasionally use nonwage sources of income to supplement factory earnings (see Table 7.5). I noted some additional income-generating activities among respondents I became more familiar with, so this practice may be more common than my data suggest. For squatter residents, additional sources of income include the earnings of a ten-year-old son as a street vendor, tortilla preparation and sale from the home, laundry service, and child care. Additional income for dormitory workers came from parents renting a small plot of land, parents who are *ejiditarios* (collective farmers), and two sets of parents who run small neighborhood groceries. Madero workers relied exclusively on industrial wages.

Whereas Ciudad Madero workers and their households are completely dependent on their factory wage, this is not true in Nogales. Wages in the new factory regime are made artificially low by several factors. First, the wage is subsidized by the prevalent practice of land invasion and squatter housing construction. Second, nonwage sources of income supplement the factory wage. Third, for dormitory residents, reproduction costs have been individualized, and daily but not intergenerational reproduction costs are met except via remittances. Finally, workers form larger households in which they can pool several incomes and renegotiate household domestic tasks. In combination, these factors, which involve an imposition of social costs onto the environment and workers' living conditions, subsidize low wages in the new factory regime.

Notes

Portions of this chapter are reprinted with permission. See Cravey, Altha J., "The Politics of Reproduction: Households in the Mexican Industrial Transition, " *Economic Geography* 73(2): 166-86. April 1997.

1. The two regional labor pools compared are not differentiated by significant ethnic differences in family/household form.

2. As of January 1, 1993, a new monetary system was established. The new unit of currency, the "new peso," is worth 1,000 of the pesos that were used up to December 31, 1992. By dropping the three zeros from the prevailing monetary values, the government endeavored to simplify record keeping and make the currency more manageable.

3· There is no universal agreement on the categorization of household types. Here, I have followed Sylvia Chant (1989), who is concerned with the relationship between household formation and political economic change.

4. The comprehensive social system of the old factory regime shares many aspects of Fordist-type national compromises found in advanced capitalist countries.

8

Conclusion

A paranoid truth at the end of the twentieth century may be closer to this: the industrialized northern border of Mexico is the prototype of a grim Taylorist future. . . . A reservoir of cheap labor is contained and channeled by the hydraulic action of an apartheid machine. The machine is increasingly indifferent to democracy on either side of the line, but not indifferent to culture, to the pouring of oil upon troubled waters. (Allan Sekula. 1997. *Dead Letter Office*, p. 32.)

Above all else, the Mexican experience demonstrates that gender is central to contemporary globalization processes. Assembly-line workers must be aware of the ways in which gender has been renegotiated at various interlocking spatial scales if they are to influence global factory regimes and improve the quality of their jobs. With this knowledge, young women and men have some of the necessary tools to build effective networks of resistance linking the spaces of the shopfloor, the household, and the community with regional or national growth spaces. The latter connections are crucial for understanding globalization from a worker's perspective because these growth spaces double as the competitive global terrain of corporate employers. Thus organizing space may be a key element for organizing resistance to the more onerous aspects of contemporary globalization.

The Mexican experience also indicates the way in which a gender logic has become tightly enmeshed with the logic and rhetoric of growth in emerging global investment zones. We have observed the ways in which gender hierarchies are contested, renegotiated and re-inscribed within high investment regions, such as northern Mexico. As the Mexican state strives to maintain the flow of foreign capital investment, it plays a pivotal role in mediating these gender contests. In the process of eliminating old forms of gender subordination, the state constructs newly gendered inequities within social and industrial policies that are reworked to promote growth. The desire for "global competitiveness" is used to justify radical changes in the organization of social reproduction and production activities. At the same time, new sources of resistance coalesce around issues of human rights, labor rights, gendered identities, and indigenous identities. Of these, one of the more sophisticated resistance movements is the ongoing Zapatista struggle, which announced its militant opposition to the North American Free Trade Agreement (NAFTA) on the first day of 1994 as the trade agreement was implemented. There is also considerable independent organizing effort within maquiladoras and other industrial workplaces, such as the ongoing struggle in 1997-98 at the Hyundai subsidiary, Han Young, in Tijuana.

The maquiladora program was an experiment that ultimately served as a model for Mexico's overall development strategy. Moreover, it became a growth prototype in the 1990s within the North American trading block and a point of leverage in subsequent global negotiations such as GATT and the Multilateral Agreement on Investments (MAI). In North America, the symbolic and functional role of the maquiladora factory regime increased throughout the 1980s and 1990s until the "free market" neoliberal model it embodies was institutionalized in 1994 with the implementation of NAFTA. Within Mexico, the factory regime that began to emerge in the 1960s in the north ultimately undercut conditions in central Mexico for both male and female workers. This process led to downward pressure on wages and benefits in the industrial, commercial, service, and informal sector throughout the country. The latest Mexican peso crisis of January 1996 and the Wall Street bailout of February 1996 have exacerbated many of the social trends documented here. These two events underscored the magnitude of social, political, and economic integration of the North American economies involved in NAFTA, while giving rise to further international pressure to maintain the gendered aspects of the maquiladora factory regime that had made it globally competitive in the first place. Mexico thus experiences more external discipline that imposes the same gender logic and social costs as before. As a result of the peso crisis and the subsequent U.S. bailout, factory managers and owners have a greater need to individualize and to lower the costs of social reproduction. This, in turn, continues to increasingly shred the social fabric.

As the Mexican maquiladora factory regime evolves at the end of the twentieth century, gender repeatedly crops up as a significant analytic and empirical detail. In early 1998, the results of a six-month-long study of NAFTA's National Administrative Office (NAO) demonstrated that export assembly transnational corporations (TNCs) regularly violate Mexican labor law by firing, harassing, and intimidating workers who become pregnant. This practice, of course, saves employers a considerable amount of money that might be spent on maternity benefits. The research also documents discrimination against pregnant workers that takes place during initial employment interviews. Young women are clearly considered productive and profitable employees, as long as they are not and do not become pregnant. Although the NAO results are a dramatic illustration of the gendering of global growth strategies, they are not likely to have widespread or immediate impact. This is because the NAO was set up by the labor side agreement of NAFTA to monitor but not enforce labor practices in each of the signatory countries.

What does the Mexican transition mean for a theoretical understanding of the relationship between capital and gender? It helps to demonstrate how tightly the two systems are bound together, such that we cannot understand many of the complexities of capitalism without scrutinizing systems of gender subordination, and vice versa. Theoretical work has provided a clear understanding of how surplus labor is extracted in production, but there is still a need to understand mechanisms of gendered exploitation, one of which is the extraction of surplus use values in domestic labor (Fraad, Resnick, and Wolff 1989; Deere 1990; Gibson and Graham 1992). As noncapitalist class relationships based on gender subordination, these micro-scale processes contribute to and help to explain larger-scale economic transformation.

How are gender, geography, and the household interrelated? The evidence from Mexico's industrial transition demonstrates that both gender and household relations are dialectically connected to the broader spaces of economic transformation. The new factory regime established itself in new regions of the country and *at the same time* restructured gender relations in both productive and reproductive activities. Industrial workers in Nogales, whether living in dormitories or squatter settlements, found themselves with a less adequate paycheck and with a reduced capacity to bargain with their employers. For Mexican industrial workers, the household nucleation thesis has been reversed. The deepening of capitalist relations and the industrialization of the northern region did not lead to a nucleation of industrial households and families. Rather than forming nuclear families, the

Nogales workers participate in subnuclear (dormitory and other room-mate) arrangements and a variety of extended forms. Much remains to be understood about daily survival within these forms and about the mechanisms of gendered exploitation that have accompanied the industrial transition. However, gender restructuring is an important component of the economic change.

Gender restructuring was crucial to the pattern and process of economic restructuring in Mexico. These gender changes are partially concealed by the complex history and transformation of Mexican industrial strategy that recently produced a new relationship between the state and the market. In the wake of the internationalization of capital, the power of the Mexican state has declined precipitously in the last two decades. The result has been a state that is subservient to capital in the way that Burawoy's "hegemonic despotism" (1985) suggests: the state now intervenes in the economy *only* to reinforce the despotism of capital. Specifically, the state acts to repress labor movements and dismantle state programs of social provision while providing concessions to attract and retain capital. Eschewing a regulatory role, the state has shifted to enforcing the rules of the marketplace, compelling the compliance of labor, and zealously clearing any obstacles in the path of capital accumulation.

As for practical consequences, the most significant finding is that social reproduction is ever more tightly bound to the employment relationship in Mexico and in contemporary TNC modes of capital accumulation. This validates Michael Burawoy's (1985) speculation about global factory regimes. It extends his argument about the close connection of production/reproduction in emerging factory regimes by showing how thoroughly gender permeates the *politics of production,* a politics that is partially displaced onto a *micropolitics of reproduction* in one contemporary global location, that is, northern Mexico.

The transformation of Mexican industrial policy from a state-led to a maquiladora strategy has rewritten the relationship between the state, the market, and the household, with dramatic consequences for the daily lives of industrial workers. Social reproduction has been reorganized simultaneously with the reorganization of production. Old channels of social provision have been replaced by community, household, and individual solutions to meet the daily needs of workers. Some goods and services that were previously provided by the state have been commodified. Housing, which formerly had been partially decommodified through INFONAVIT and other union-sponsored housing programs, now has been completely recommodified in the maquiladora factory regime.

The transition to the new factory regime is complex, however, because some of the goods previously provided by the state are being provided now by the *employer*. These goods include health care (in some cases), housing (in the form of single-sex dormitories), and child care. This reorganization of social reproduction has dramatically changed the balance of power in the employee/employer relationship in favor of the employer, and has thus consequently made workers more vulnerable to the demands of their employers.

The Mexican industrial transition has been facilitated by a restructuring of gender relations, both in the workplace and in the domestic sphere. The male industrial worker of the earlier factory regime has been supplanted by a younger female workforce. Less visible but no less important to this transition has been the restructuring of gender relations in the household and in the private lives of workers. The predominantly nuclear household form supported by a male breadwinner, which was the norm in the state-led factory regime, has given way to a multiplicity of forms in which workers devise new strategies for survival.

Several processes operate in the new factory regime that subsidize and depress the wages of maquiladora workers. One of the best-documented is the pooling of multiple wages in restructured households to meet reproductive needs. This research demonstrates that land invasion and squatter settlement have a similar effect on wages. Communities of workers organize themselves and claim homesites in the *colonias populares* to supply their own housing outside of the formal market and at minimal cost. In addition to these processes, some Nogales workers have nonwage sources of income, which also serve to depress factory wages.

In conjunction with the reconstitution and reorganization of the household unit the increased participation of women in waged work has had an impact on the division of domestic labor. Whereas men in Ciudad Madero relied almost exclusively on the labor of their wives to tend to their reproductive needs, these tasks are often renegotiated in Nogales. Child care has been the arena of the most dramatic change, with some Nogales men contributing labor *on a regular basis* through a sequential scheduling strategy. Men in Nogales also may help with cooking, laundry, and grocery shopping in a more systematic fashion than in Ciudad Madero.

The company-run dormitories in Nogales are a novel form of household in Mexico, reflecting the increased power and control of employers over their employees. For workers who must accept this control, both productive and reproductive activities are strictly regulated by their transnational employers, resulting in a loss of autonomy and privacy. The dormitory system subsidizes wages within the maquiladora factory regime in several ways. Since social reproduction is organized on an individual basis within the dorms, the cost is minimized. Also, the employer can extend the discipline of the factory into the dormitory, adjusting the size of the workforce when necessary.

The Mexican experience demonstrates the profound impact the state, particularly a developmentalist state, can have on labor organizing. The intimate alliance between the Mexican state and the labor unions in the mid-twentieth century affected the internal organizational structure of both the unions and their national confederations, as well as the regulation of workplace relations and the daily practice of collective representation. The centralization of power that occurred during the parallel process of state-building and unionization from 1930 to 1976 was a great source of strength for unionists. In the 1970s and 1980s, the geographical shift northward and the dispersion of industrial sites allowed the state to reverse industrial policy. This national development strategy has presented workers and the labor union movement with a knotty dilemma. Labor unionists must find new ways and new spaces in which to reinvent themselves.

A geographical shift in production during the 1970s and 1980s was clearly useful to the Mexican state, which aligned itself with transnational employers to establish a radically different factory regime in dispersed northern locations distant from Mexico City. This new regime involved a renegotiation of the national gender contract. Gender struggles within households, neighborhoods, and workplaces of the new factory regime became institutionalized in Mexican economic and social policy. Subsequently, the new factory regime was used to undercut the state/labor alliance, which was strongest in centralized production sites (i.e., in and near Mexico City) and which had characterized the years of import substitution industrialization. In some superficial ways, this alliance still appears to be intact—the main official labor group, the CTM, still wields a measure of power at the national level and still binds a significant percentage of workers to the PRI's official party structure. However, as the Nogales case study illustrates, the labor federation has taken contradictory positions. In that context of extreme vulnerability, local labor leaders collaborated with local political and business leaders to stifle grassroots organizing efforts in 1980 and to contain future complaints within the local jurisdiction. Workers in Nogales have had to find alternatives to the official labor unions in order to attend to the most basic workplace issues.

Decentralization of political and union power has also weakened the union movement in Mexico, but this particular spatial change may have unintended consequences in the future. It could be that the decentralization of bargaining structures and regulatory structures will become a useful tool for labor and community organizers, because the increasingly diffuse pattern of struggle will be more difficult for the hierarchical centralized CTM to control. In the Nogales case study, however, decentralization worked to the short-term advantage of the transnational employers, whose tightly disciplined manager enclave used sociospatial arrangements to circumscribe and contain potential protests while establishing systems of labor control that reinforce corporate dominance—with the most extreme form of the latter occurring in the crowded single-sex dormitories where twenty-four-hour guards regulate the most intimate aspects of the lives of workers. In these former factory buildings, the spaces of resistance have been reduced in scope but nevertheless persist as important sites of struggle. Likewise, neighborhood-based community organizing provides an alternate space in which to raise gender and labor issues that have resulted from a decentralized geographical pattern. These sorts of micro-spaces may be useful locations for organizing resistance to the new labor practices because they are less subject to centralized control. For instance, the new spaces of the corporate dormitory, while highly regulated and repressive, may engender an innovative culture that will influence the trajectory of the local factory regime.

One way that women, community organizers, and labor unionists are beginning to confront the new production regime is through transnational labor solidarity and linking workplace struggles with community issues. As the two economies have become more closely integrated, numerous connections have been established between Mexican and U.S. labor unionists. These enlarge the scope of labor union struggles beyond the locality and beyond the boundaries of the nation. In Mexico, many of the workers who have created transnational alliances are located in northern and north-central parts of the country. A common employer often serves as the basis for an initial contact between worker groups in the two countries.

These recent examples hint at the potential *usefulness of space* in redefining the terms of union struggles to recover the power that Mexican workers lost in the reversal of industrial policy two decades ago. These developments are only suggestive, but may indicate that by enlarging the scope of the struggle, Mexican labor unionists may regain a measure of influence over the geography of production. The new types of production in the northern region are opening spaces for new types of labor militancy that will not be supervised by the CTM. Whatever emerges in the future, however, workers and labor unionists must chart a difficult path, because the central labor movement's historical alliance with the Mexican state has been a source of strength and, more recently, a source of weakness. It remains to be seen whether workers have the political will to renegotiate or transcend their alliance with the "dinosaurs"[1] and other conservative elements of political leadership in the Mexican state. The task is all the more treacherous in the intensely competitive global environment of the 1990s, in which the factories at the expanding frontier of job creation in northern Mexico must compete in a complex new spatial dynamic that places them in competition with U.S. sites, as well as many other low-wage sites throughout the industrializing world.

Understanding the gendered nature of this challenge is crucial and requires a geographical sensibility. Why is this so? Precisely because micro-scale negotiations over the gender division of labor within households and neighborhoods influence global and regional dynamics. At the same time, national policies and global competitions influence the gendered balance of power at the micro-scale. As the Mexican evidence demonstrates, gender struggles can move between various spatial scales in unpredictable and complex ways. As we have seen, gender contests in one arena may, and probably will, reemerge in other spaces. Workers in global factories who are able to see the connections between the spaces of the shopfloor, the household, and the neighborhood have much to teach us about how to move toward a socially just future. The conditions in global growth zones such as northern Mexico highlight some of the general trends we may anticipate if we ignore their experience. A better alternative would be to actively construct worker strategies that are versatile enough to link micro-scale politics with regional and global gender dynamics.

Notes

1. Mexico's political leadership has shown increasing signs of fragmentation in the last few years. The most traditional group, as distinguished from the foreign-educated *técnicos*, is frequently referred to as "*los dinosaurios*," to underscore a popular notion that they are relics of the past.

Appendix

The analysis here is based on in-depth interviews conducted in 1992 with sixty workers about their work life and about the organization of their households. Samples were chosen to provide a comparison between households of the old factory regime and two distinct types of households in the new factory regime, where a rich variety of household forms are emerging. The specific groups used in the study include: (1) industrial worker households in Ciudad Madero; (2) the typical industrial worker households in Nogales squatter communities; and (3) the less typical single-sex households in the company-run worker dormitories of the new factory regime.

A rough quota system (and random samples within these quotas) was used to obtain a representative sample from the three groups. Quotas were defined prior to informant selection by geographic boundaries, and subsample size was weighted to reflect the distribution of industrial employment and residence. The first group was selected randomly from two major industries in Ciudad Madero: a medium-sized, privately owned processing plant for magnesium oxide (Quimica del Mar) and a large, state-run petroleum enterprise (PEMEX). The second group of workers was chosen from four different *colonias populares* (squatter communities) in Nogales in three distinct parts of the town: a central industrial district, a large undeveloped area beyond the periphery road west of town, and a hillside overlooking the main thoroughfare and business district. The third group was chosen randomly from five separate Nogales dormitories: Sonitronies' (an organization supplying labor to twenty factories) female dorms #3 and #7, Sonitronies' male dorm #6, Wilson Jones (a paper products maquiladora) female dorm, and Wilson Jones' male dorm. Because I was denied access to the dorms, I was forced to adapt my sampling strategy by waiting outside for residents to leave or return to request their participation.

The central objective of this study is to explore the changing relationship between the state, market, and household in the context of Third World industrialization. To this end, the research attempts to uncover the ways in which the relationship between the state and maquiladora workers demonstrates a reduced state commitment to social welfare. In turn, I explore how the families and households of maquiladora workers have compensated for this state retrenchment. They frequently adjust the size and composition of their households, but they also devise new strategies for meeting important needs (e.g., housing and health care).

In an effort to understand the effect of the industrial transition on daily life, the research explores the organization of daily social reproduction in the household. This examination along with the previous examination on household formation provides the basis for a household-level comparison between the old and new factory regimes. In addition, two very different household forms within the new regime are compared–squatter households and single-sex dormitories.

Methodology

The research uses an intensive case study method to combine interview and archival research with participant observation. By linking direct observation and systematic interviewing with many historical techniques, we can fashion a flexible method that combines the use of multiple sources of evidence.

The work is based on fieldwork in Mexico, conducted between October 1991 and September 1992. Virtually all of the year was spent in Nogales, Sonora, which was chosen for three characteristics that both make it unique and make the Nogales labor pool particularly vulnerable. First, there are no active labor unions in Nogales maquiladoras: neither official nor unofficial unions (Carrillo 1985). Union membership rates in other cities with maquiladoras, by contrast, range from 15 to 100 percent (Carrillo 1983, 11). Second, a much higher proportion of Nogales' workers are employed by the industry than elsewhere (Perlo Cohen 1987, 160; Sánchez 1990a). Third, Nogales has several worker dormitories where young workers live without their families. This type of housing does not exist elsewhere in the maquiladora industry (Denman 1991; Feagin 1991).

Ciudad Madero, Tamaulipas, was a secondary field site that serves to represent the previous period of state-led industrialization. Ciudad Madero was chosen in order to provide a contrast with the maquiladora factory regime. Petroleum production, the main economic activity in the region, is state-owned by Petroleos Mexicanos, PEMEX. In Ciudad Madero and other earlier industrial centers, abundant state funds were allocated to health, education, and other needs of the community (Grayson 1989). Therefore, the two sites provide a stark contrast in terms of production, household form, and the organization of social reproduction.

A deliberately non-random sampling technique was used to select informants. This method is well-suited to qualitative questions which seek to understand underlying relationships between phenomena (Bulmer and Warwick 1983; Merriam 1988). Merriam (1988) states that "non-probability sampling is the method of choice in qualitative case studies." The principal weakness of this sampling strategy is that one cannot use the data to make generalizations in the statistical sense (Bulmer and Warwick 1983). For the comparison of the three groups of workers, I altered the sampling strategy, using a rough quota system to randomize the sample, as explained below.

My methodology is similar to that used by Benería and Roldan (1987) to investigate industrial homeworkers in Mexico City. They combined a "partial participant observation" with intensive formal and informal interviews. Based on their research questions and personal contacts that they were able to make at the beginning of their fieldwork, they chose purposive, non-random samples of homeworkers to interview. They made several visits to their informants and consulted with them over interpretive problems. Benería and Roldan also toured the production processes and interviewed representatives in a non-random sample of firms. Using their intensive research design as a model allowed me some flexibility in the design itself.

The comparison between the state-led factory regime of Ciudad Madero and the maquiladora factory regime is based on interviews with three distinct groups of workers: (1) industrial workers employed in public and private enterprises in Ciudad Madero; (2) Nogales maquiladora workers living in squatter housing; and (3) Nogales maquiladora workers living in company-run dormitories. All workers were interviewed with a structured set of questions. This facilitated comparison on such variables as household composition, the percent of income devoted to food and shelter, percent of income contributed to the family, experience with state or factory health care, and degree of control over free time.

The interviews themselves took place under widely varied circumstances due to problems of access to certain worker groups, particularly the dormitory residents. The primary respondent was in all cases a person (of either sex) who identified himself as an industrial worker. However, other members of the household were encouraged to participate in the discussion and to contribute their perspectives and opinions separately. For this reason, the household itself was the preferred location for interviews. Unfortunately I was denied access to the dormitories, so I was forced to contact these workers in the street outside the buildings. These interviews consequently took place in a nearby restaurant or on a public sidewalk, depending on the preference of the interviewee. In Ciudad Madero, workers in private enterprises were interviewed at their place of work, because their residential dispersion made household interviews impractical.

This study is based on in-depth interviews with sixty workers about their work life and about the organization of their households. The interview questionnaire is included in the appendix. Three distinct groups of worker households are compared in this study: (1) industrial worker households of Ciudad Madero; (2) industrial worker households of Nogales squatter communities; and (3) single-sex households in company-run worker dormitories of the maquiladora period of industrialization. These samples provide a comparison between households of the state-led factory regime (group 1) and two distinct types of households of the maquiladora regime: the diverse unregulated (group 2) and the highly regulated (group 3).

A rough quota system in conjunction with random samples within these quotas was used to obtain a representative sample for these three groups. The quotas were either defined by geographical boundaries or by worker activity, as explained below.

The first group were selected randomly from two industries in Ciudad Madero: six workers from a privately owned processing plant for magnesium oxide, Quimica del Mar and fourteen from a state-run petroleum enterprise, PEMEX. The process of selection for the industries was quite different because I was allowed access to the Quimica del Mar workers within the factory. For the randomization there, the manager and I identified six different parts of the plant from which to select an informant. At PEMEX, I was not allowed to interview workers, so I randomized the sample by selecting individuals from eight-block units in the city. More workers from PEMEX were interviewed because the company employs a majority of the city's industrial workforce, far more than the local private industries.[1]

The second group of workers were chosen from four different *colonias populares* (squatter communities) in Nogales (Figure 5.1). The process of randomization was again based on geographical quotas, such that distinct squatter communities and distinct units within these were chosen before the informant selection was made. Seven workers were selected from Los Tápiros, seven from Los Encinos, five from Artículo Vientesiete and one from Tierra Y Liberdad; larger random samples were taken from larger neighborhoods. These colonias represent three distinct parts of town: a central industrial district; a large undeveloped area beyond the periphery road to the west of town; and a hillside overlooking the main thoroughfare and business district, respectively.

The third group were chosen randomly from five separate Nogales dormitories: four workers from Sonitronies' (an organization supplying labor to twenty factories) dorm #3, four workers from Sonitronies' dorm #7, five workers from Sonitronies' male dorm #6, three workers from Wilson Jones's (a paper products maquiladora) female dorm, and four workers from Wilson Jones's male dorm. In this case, I was denied access to the dorms so I waited outside for residents to leave or return to the dorm in order to request their participation. Once again, the sub-sample size was weighted by the population size of the residence so that larger samples were taken from more populous dormitories.

In all instances, the interviewee was a person who identified him- or herself as an industrial worker. The sex of the respondent was noted but was not a criteria used in the selection process. In the case of the dormitory residents (group 3), however, the quotas for various dorms effectively determined the sex ratio of the sample because all dorms had either male or female residents. The sample of dormitory residents included nine male and eleven female workers. The sample of Ciudad Madero workers (group 1) was composed of fifteen men and five women. Nogales squatter residents (group 2) were represented by a sample of eight men and twelve women.

Questionnaire (in English)

This information will be used in my research. It will not be used for any other purpose. If any question is too personal or you don't want to answer it just say so.
1. Who are the members of your household/family and what are their relationships?

2. How long have you lived here? Where did you live before?
3. How much schooling have you had?
4. Where are you employed? How long have you been there?
5. Who else in your household is employed? Where?
6. What other sources of income does your family or household have?
7. How is water delivered to your household? What does it cost? Who pays?
8. Who buys and prepares food? How far away is the store?
9. Who does the laundry? How much time is involved?
10. Who cares for the children?
11. Where do you go for health care?
12. Who cares for you when you are sick? Who cares for the other workers when they are sick?
13. What would happen if you lost your job? In the factory where you work, what happens when a worker becomes pregnant?
14. What is your income? How much money do you contribute to your household?
15. What is the percentage of income contributed to the family?
16. How much is your rent? (How much rent do you pay to the owner of the dormitory? Does this sum pay for anything besides the sleeping space?) How much are your food expenses? What percentage of your income is spent on housing and food?
17. Does your household/family have other ways of earning income?
18. Does your employer provide any services to your family such as child care, laundry facilities, purified water?
19. Do you receive any government services other than social security and education?

Questionnaire (in Spanish)

La informacion es para mi tesis. No lo usare en otra manera. Dime por favor, si una pregunta es demasiado personal.
1. ?Qienes son los miembros de su casa? ?Cuales son sus relaciones y edades?
2. ?Cuanto tiempo tiene de vivir aqui? ?Donde vivió antes?
3. ?Hasta qué año de estudios llegó usted?
4. ?Donde trabaja usted? ?Que tiempo tiene de trabajar?
5. ?Trabajan otros miembros de su casa? ?Donde trabajan?
6. ?Cuales otras fuentes de ingreso tienen su familia o su casa?
7. ?Como obtienen ustedes agua por la casa (en el dormitorio)? Cuanto cuesta? ?Qiene paga (costea)?

8. ?Quiene compra los alimentos y quienes preparan las comidas? Esta lejos la tienda de abarrotes?
9. ?Quiene lava la ropa en su casa? Cuanto tiempo invierte en lavar ropa?
10. ?Quién cuida a los ninos en su casa?
11. ?Quién les da servicio médico?
12. ?Quien le cuida cuando esta enferma? ?Quien le cuida de los otros trabajadores cuando ellos estan enfermos?
13. ?Que sucederia si usted pierde el trabajo? En la fabrica donde trabaja usted (Avent, GE, etc), que sucederia cuando una trabajadora esta embarazada?
14. ?Cuanto gana en la fábrica? ?Cuanto aporta para la casa?
15. ?Que porcentaje de su ingreso contribuye a la familia/casa?
16. ?Cuanto paga de renta? (*Cuanto le da a el dueno del dormitorio? Esta suma es de acuerdo a la ubicacion y que mas?*) Cuantos son sus gastos de alimentacion cada semana? ?Qué porcentaje de su ingreso contribuye a la renta? Y a la alimentacion?
17. ?Tiene su familia otra maneras de gana ingreso?
18. ?Proporciona su patron (de la fabrica) algunos servicios a su familia, como agua purificada o guarderia de ninos o facilidades para lavar ropa?
19. ?Recibe usted algunos servicios del gobierno ademas de seguro social y educacion?

Notes

1. In 1990, Pemex employed 64 percent of the Madero industrial workers according to Censo General de Población. Tamaulipas.

Bibliography

Primary Sources

Alfaro Zavalo, Juan. Nogales squatter resident. Personal interview. May 23, 1992.

Alonso Morales, Raúl. STPRM official. Personal interview. July 28, 1992.

Aviles, Patricia. Nogales squatter resident. Personal interview. May 17, 1992.

Bietel, Tim. Manager, General Electric. Personal interview. February 6, 1992.

Carrasco, Carlos. Nogales squatter resident and former dormitory resident. Personal interview. January 14, 1992.

Delgado, Ramón. Nogales dormitory resident. Personal interview. May 3, 1992.

Denman, Catalina. Professor, El Colegio de Sonora. Hermosillo, Mexico. Personal interview. July 23, 1991.

Diaz Aguayo, Alejandro. IMSS doctor specializing in occupational health. Personal interview. July 9, 1992.

Enrique Ortega, Tomás. Nogales squatter resident. Personal interview. May 23, 1992.

Enriques Ramírez, David. PEMEX worker. Personal interview. July 30, 1992.

Feagin, Ed. AFL-CIO official, Washington, D.C. Personal interview. July 19, 1991.

Fernández, Antonio. Worker at Quimica del Mar. Personal interview. July 30, 1992.

Franco, Concepción. Secretary, Junta de Conciliación. Personal interview. September 14, 1992.

Fraser, Don. Manager, ITT maquiladora. Personal interview. May 12, 1992.

Guerrero, Isabel. Director, Centro Contra La Violencia. Personal interview. March 6, 1992.

Gutiérrez, Enrique. Nogales dormitory resident. Personal interview. May 17, 1992.

Hernández Navarette, Ana. Nogales squatter resident. Personal interview. March 30, 1992.

Herrera, Manuel. Nogales dormitory resident. Personal interview. May 10, 1992.

Higgins, Tom. Manager, Wilson Jones maquiladora. Personal interview. March 19, 1992.

Hinojosa, Luis. PEMEX worker. Personal interview. July 30, 1992.

Hurtado, Raúl. Nogales dormitory resident. Personal interview. May 23, 1992.

Infante Alvarez, Retired electrician from PEMEX and Chronicler of Ciudad Madero. Personal interview, July 29, 1992

Kamp, Richard. Director, Border Ecology Project. Personal interview. February 5, 1992.

Laituri, Melinda. Researcher, University of Northern Colorado. Personal interview. August 12, 1992.

Leal, Teresa. Social activist in Nogales. Personal interview. February 24, 1992. November 11, 1991.

López, Marisa. Nogales dormitory resident. Personal interview. May 10, 1992.

Medina, Maria Teresa. PEMEX worker. Personal interview. July 30, 1992.

Molina Flores, Jorge. Retired PEMEX worker. Personal interview. July 23, 1992.

Monroy Aguilar, Mónica. Nogales dormitory resident. Personal interview. March 28, 1992.

Ortiz Mora, Laura. Nogales squatter resident. Personal interview. May 17, 1992.

Ramírez Quijano, Fernando. Medical doctor at PEMEX hospital in Ciudad Madero. Personal interview. August 5, 1992.

Rigoli, Al. Director of Sales, Collectron-Sonitronies. Personal interview. May 12, 1992.

Rios Bohorquez, Domingo. Nogales dormitory resident. Personal interview. May 10, 1992.

Rodriguez Gonzalez, Oscar. Manager at Quimica del Mar. Personal interview. July 30, 1992.

Sáenz, Maria Elena. Nogales dormitory resident. Personal interview. March 28, 1992.

Salcedo, Roberto. PEMEX worker. Personal interview. July 25, 1992.

Sánchez, Gabriel. Quimica del Mar worker. Personal interview. July 30, 1992.

Serrano, Mercedes. Nogales squatter resident. Personal interview, March 16, 1992.

Valdés, Alfredo. Retired PEMEX worker. Personal interview, July 29, 1992.

Zamora, Elena. Nogales dormitory resident. Personal interview. May 2, 1992.

Zatarain Rojo. Director, IMSS Guardería (IMSS Child Care Center). Personal interview. July 16, 1992.

Secondary Sources

Abramovitz, Mimi. 1988. *Regulating the Lives of Women: Social Welfare Policy from Colonial Times to the Present*. Boston: South End Press.

Aguilar, Marian Angela. 1990. "Mexico," in John Dixon and Robert P. Scheurell (eds.), *Social Welfare in Latin America*. London: Routledge.

Aguilar Camín, Héctor and Pablo González Cassanova. coords. 1987. *México ante la Crisis*. 3rd ed. Mexico D.F.: Siglo Veintiuno Editores.

Alarcón, Diana and Terry McKinley. 1992. "Beyond Import Substitution: The Restructuring Projects of Mexico and Brazil," *Latin American Perspectives* 19(2): 72-87.

Amado, Jose Daniel. 1989. "Free Industrial Zones: Law and Industrial Development in the New International Division of Labor," *University of Pennsylvania Journal of International Business Law* 11(1): 81-150.

Amin, Samir. 1976. *Unequal Development*. London: Monthly Review Press.

Amsden, Alice H. 1989. *Asia's Next Giant: South Korea and Late Industrialization*. Oxford: Oxford University Press.

———. 1990. "Third World Industrialization: 'Global Fordism' or a New Model?" *New Left Review* (1990): 5-31.

———. 1992. "A Theory of Government Intervention in Late Industrialization," in L. Putterman and D. Rueschemeyer (eds.), *The State and the Market in Development*. Boulder, Colo.: Lynne Rienner Publishers, Inc.

Anaya Nieves, Jose. 1974. "Un Pueblo que Supo Luchar por su Independencia, para No Sucumbir," *Revista Tamaulipas* 230: 56-59.

Anzaldúa, G. 1987. *Borderlands : the New Mestiza = La Frontera*. San Francisco, Spinsters/Aunt Lute.

Arenal, Sandra. 1986. *Sangre Joven: Las Maquiladoras por Dentro*. México: Editorial Nuestro Tiempo.

Arrom, Silvia Marina. 1985. *The Women of Mexico City, 1790-1857*. Stanford: Stanford University Press.

Balassa, Bela. 1981. *The Newly Industrializing Countries in the World Economy*. New York: Pergamon.

———. 1988. "The Lessons of East Asian Development, an Overview," *Economic Development and Cultural Change* 36: 273-290.

Baran, Paul A. 1957. *The Political Economy of Growth*. New York: Monthly Review Press.

Barkin, David. 1990. *Distorted Development: Mexico in the World Economy*. Boulder, Colo.: Westview Press.

Barrett, Richard E. and Soomi Chin. 1987. "Export-Oriented Industrializing States in the Capitalist World System: Similarities and Differences," in Deyo,

Frederic. C. (ed.), *The Political Economy of the New Asian Industrialism* (pp. 23-43). Ithaca: Cornell University Press.

Barry, Tom, ed. 1992. *Mexico: A Country Guide*. Albuquerque: Center for Inter-Hemispheric Education Resource Center.

Bello, Walden and Stephanie Rosenfeld. 1990. *Dragons in Distress: Asia's Miracle Economies in Crisis*. San Francisco: The Institute for Food and Development Policy.

Benería, Lourdes. 1992. "The Mexican Debt Crisis: Restructuring the Economy and the Household," in Lourdes Benería and Shelley Feldman (eds.), *Unequal Burden: Economic Crises, Persistent Poverty and Women's Work* (pp. 83-104). Boulder, Colo.: Westview Press.

Benería, Lourdes and Martha Roldán. 1987. *The Crossroads of Class and Gender: Industrial Homework, Subcontracting, and Household Dynamics in Mexico City*. Chicago: The University of Chicago Press.

Benería, Lourdes and Gita Sen. 1982. "Class and Gender Inequalities and Women's Role in Economic Development–Theoretical and Practical Implications," *Feminist Studies* 8(1): 157-176.

Blomstrom, Magnus and Bjorn Hettne. 1984. *Development Theory in Transition: The Dependency Debate and Beyond: Third World Responses*. London: Zed Books.

Borzutzky, Silvia. 1993. "Social Security and Health Policies in Latin America: The Changing Roles of the State and Private Sector," *Latin American Research Review* 28(2): 246-256.

Bowlby, Sophie. 1990. "Women, Work and the Factory: Control and Constraints," *Geography* 76(75): 17-26.

Bowlby, Sophie, Jane Lewis; Linda McDowell, and Jo Foord. 1989. "The Geography of Gender," in Richard Peet and Nigel Thrift (eds.), *New Models in Geography*, vol. 2 (pp. 157-175). London: Unwin Hyman.

Braverman, Harry. 1974. *Labor and Monopoly Capital*. New York: Monthly Review Press.

Brenner, R. 1977. "The Origins of Capitalist Development: A Critique of Neo-Smithian Marxism," *New Left Review* 104: 25-92.

Briseño, Jaime Aguilar. 1988. "Plan 'Lazaro Cardenas:' Breve Historia del GURNH de la Seccion 1 del SRTPRM." *Revista Tamaulipas* (special edition: 50th Aniversary of the Nationalization of Petroleum), pp. 65-76.

Browett, J. G. 1986. "Industrialization in the Global Periphery: The Significance of the Newly Industrializing Countries of East and Southeast Asia," *Environment and Planning D: Society and Space* 4(4): 401-418.

Brydon, Lynne and Sylvia Chant. 1989. *Women in the Third World: Gender Issues in Rural and Urban Areas*. New Brunswick: Rutgers University Press.

Bulmer, Martin and Donald P. Warwick, eds. 1983. *Social Research in Developing Countries: Surveys and Censuses in the Third World.* Chichester: John Wiley and Sons.

Burawoy, Michael. 1985. *The Politics of Production: Factory Regimes under Capitalism and Socialism.* London: Verso.

Bustamente, Jorge A. 1983. "Maquiladoras: A New Face of International Capitalism on Mexico's Northern Frontier," in June Nash and Maria Patricia Fernández-Kelly (eds.), *Women, Men and the International Division of Labor.* Albany: State University of New York Press.

Canak, William L. 1984. "The Peripheral State Debate: State Capitalist and Bureaucratic-Authoritarian Regimes in Latin America," *Latin American Research Review* 19(1): 3-36.

Canclini, Nestor Garcia. 1995. Hybrid Cultures: Strategies for Entering and Leaving Modernity. Minneapolis, Minn. : University of Minnesota Press.

Cardoso, F. H. and E. Faletto. 1979. *Dependency and Development in Latin America.* Berkeley: University of California Press.

Carnegie Quarterly. 1991. "Promoting Binational Cooperation to Improve Health along the U.S.-Mexico Border: When Research Pays Off for the Community," *Carnegie Quarterly* (Winter-Fall): 1-8.

Carrillo V., Jorge. 1983. "Crisis in the Labor Movement on the Northern Mexico Border," *International Report* 1: 10-12.

———. 1985. *Conflictos Laborales en la Industria Maquiladora.* Tijuana: Centro de Estudios Fronterizos del Norte de Mexico.

———. 1991. "The Evolution of the Maquiladora Industry: Labor Relations in a New Context," in Kevin J. Middlebrook (ed.), *Unions, Workers and the State in Mexico* (pp. 213-231). San Diego: Center for U.S.–Mexican Studies.

Carrillo V., Jorge and Alberto Hernández. 1985. *Mujeres Fronterizas en la Industria Maquiladora.* México: SEP/CEFNOMEX.

Carrillo V., Jorge and Mónica Jasis. 1983. "La Salud y La Mujer Obrera en las Plantas Maquiladoras, El Caso de Tijuana," *Enfermería Hoy* 4 (June): 20-33.

Chant, Sylvia. 1985a. "Single Parent Families: Choice or Constraint? The Formation of Female-Headed Households in Mexican Shanty Towns," *Development and Change* 16: 635-656.

———. 1985b. "Family Formation and Female Roles in Querétaro, Mexico," *Bulletin of Latin American Research* 4: 17-32.

———. 1989. "Gender and the Urban Household," in Lynne Brydon and Sylvia Chant (eds.), *Women in the Third World: Gender Issues in Rural and Urban Areas* (pp. 134-160). New Brunswick: Rutgers University Press.

———. 1991. *Women and Survival in Mexican Cities: Perspectives on Gender, Labour Markets and Low-Income Households.* Manchester and New York: Manchester University Press.

Chant, Sylvia and Peter Ward. 1987. "Family Structure and Low-Income Housing Policy." *Third World Planning Review* 9(1): 5-19.

Chapkis, Wendy and Cynthia Enloe. 1983. *Of Common Cloth*. Washington, D.C.: Transactional Institute.

Cho, S. K. 1985. "The Dilemmas of Export-Led Industrialization: South Korea and the World Economy," *Berkeley Journal of Sociology* 30: 63-94.

Chrispin, Barbara R. 1990. "Employment and Manpower Development in the Maquiladora Industry: Reaching Maturity," in Khosrow Fatemi (ed.), *The Maquiladora Industry: Economic Solution or Problem?* (pp. 71-90). New York: Praeger.

Christopherson Susan. 1983a. *Family and Class in the New Industrial City*. Ph.D. dissertation. University of California, Berkeley.

———. 1983b. "The Household and Class Formation: Determinants of Residential Location in Ciudad Juárez," *Environment and Planning D: Society and Space* 1(3): 323-338.

Clark, Gordon. 1989. *Unions and Communities under Siege*. Cambridge: Cambridge University Press.

Clark, Marjorie R. 1934. *Organized Labor in Mexico*. Chapel Hill: University of North Carolina Press.

Cline, William. 1982. "Can the East Asian Model be Generalized?" *World Development* 10: 81-90.

Cockcroft, James. 1983. *Mexico: Class Formation, Capital Accumulation and the State*. New York: Monthly Review Press.

Connell, R. W. 1994. "The State, Gender and Sexual Politics: Theory and Appraisal," in H. L. Radtke and H. J. Stam (eds.), *Power/Gender* (pp. 136-173). London: Sage Publications.

Cook, M. L. 1994. Regional Integration and Transnational Labor Strategies under NAFTA. *Proceedings of a Conference on Regional Integration and Industrial Relations in North America*, New York School of Industrial Relations, Cornell University.

Cook, Maria Lorena and Kevin Middlebrook and Juan Molinar Horcasitas, eds. 1994. *The Politics of Economic Restructuring: State-Society Relations and Regime Change in Mexico*. San Diego: Center for U.S.-Mexican Studies.

Corbridge, Stuart. 1986. *Capitalist World Development: A Critique of Radical Development Geography*. Totowa, N.J.: Rowman & Littlefield.

———. 1993. *Debt and Development*. Oxford: Blackwell Publishers.

Cornelius, Wayne A., Ann L. Craig and Jonathon Fox, eds. 1994. *Transforming State-Society Relations in Mexico: The National Solidarity Strategy*. San Diego: Center for US-Mexican Studies.

Corro, Salvador and Jose Reveles. 1989. *La Quina: El Lado Oscuro del Poder*. Mexico: Editorial Planeta Mexicana.

Cravey, Altha J. 1993. The Changing Relationship of the State, Market and Household: Industrial Strategies in Mexico. Ph.D. dissertation., Department of Geography, University of Iowa, Iowa City.

———. 1998. "Cowboys and Dinosaurs: Mexican Trade Unionism and the State," in Andrew Herod (ed.) *Organizing the Landscape: Labor Unionism in Geographical Perspective* (pp. 75-98). Minneapolis: University of Minnesota Press.

Crow, Ben and Alan Thomas. 1983. *Third World Atlas*. Milton Keynes: Open University Press.

Cumings, Bruce. 1987. "The Origins and Development of the Northeast Asian Political Economy: Industrial Sectors, Product Cycles, and Political Consequences," in Frederic Deyo (ed.), *The Political Economy of New Asian Industrialization* (pp. 44-83). Ithaca: Cornell University Press.

Cypher, James M. 1990. *State and Capital in Mexico: Development Policy since 1940*. Boulder, Colo.: Westview Press.

Datos Generales de la Refineria Madero. 1982. Mexico: PEMEX.

Deere, Carmen Diana. 1990. *Household and Class Relations: Peasants and Landlords in Northern Peru*. Berkeley: University of California Press.

de Janvry, Alain. 1981. *The Agrarian Question and Reformism in Latin America*. Baltimore: The Johns Hopkins University Press.

de la Garza, E. 1993. *Restructuracion Productiva y Respuesta Sindical en México*. Mexico City: Universidad Autónoma de México, Instituto de Investigaciones Económicas.

Denman, Catalina. 1988. "Repercusiónes de la Industria Maquiladora de Exportación en la Salud: El Peso al Nacer de Hijos de Obreras en Nogales." Masters thesis. El Colegio de Sonora.

———. 1990. "Tiempos Modernos: Trabaja y Morir (Tóxicos en la Maquila)," en F. Mora y V. M. Reynoso (coords.), *Modernización y Legislación Laboral en el Noroeste De Mexico*. Memorias del Foro del Mismo Nombre. El Colegio de Sonora. Universidad de Sonora. Fundación Friedrich Ebert. Hermosillo.

Denman, Catalina y J. Armando Haro. 1991. *Evaluación de la Atención Primaria a la Salud de la Frontera Sonorense: El Caso de Nogales: Reporte Final de Investigación*. Linea de Salud y Sociedad. El Colegio de Sonora.

Denzin, Norman K. 1982. *The Research Act: A Theoretical Introduction to Sociological Methods*. New York: McGraw-Hill.

Deyo, Frederic C., ed. 1987. *The Political Economy of the New Asian Industrialism*. Ithaca: Cornell University Press.

——— 1989. *Beneath the Miracle: Labor Subordination in the New Asian Industrialism*. Berkeley: University of California Press.

———. 1990. "Economic Policy and the Popular Sector," in Gary Gereffi and Donald Wyman (eds.), *Manufacturing Miracles: Paths of Industrialization in Latin America and East Asia* (pp. 179-204). Princeton: Princeton University Press.

156   WOMEN AND WORK IN MEXICO'S MAQUILADORAS

"Documentos Historicos: Sobre la Huelga de los Trabajadores de la Compania Petroleo El Aguila en 1924." 1988. *Revista Tamaulipas* (special edition), pp. 55-59.

Dunbier, Roger. 1968. *The Sonoran Desert: Its Geography, Economy and People.* Tucson: The University of Arizona Press.

Duncan, Simon. 1994. "Theorising Differences in Patriarchy." *Environment and Planning A* 26(8): 1177-1194.

Elson, Diane and Ruth Pearson. 1981. "The Subordination of Women and the Internationalization of Factory Production," in Kate Young, Carol Wolkowitz, and Roslyn Mccullagh (eds.), *Of Marriage and the Market: Women's Subordination Internationally and Its Lessons* (pp. 18-40). London: Routledge.

"Epoca del Auge Petrolero en Tampico." 1988. *Revista Tamaulipas, Album de Oro. Edición Especial.* 50° Aniversario de la Nacionalización del Petroleo, pp. 42-43.

Evans, Peter. 1979. *Dependent Development: The Alliance of Multinational, State and Local Capital in Brazil.* Princeton, N.J.: Princeton University Press.

——— 1987. "Class, State and Dependence in East Asia: Lessons for Latin Americanists," in Frederic. C. Deyo (ed.), *The Political Economy of the New Asian Industrialism* (pp. 203-226). Ithaca: Cornell University Press.

———. 1992. "The State As Problem and Solution: Predation, Embedded Autonomy, and Structural Change," in Stephan Haggard and Robert R. Kaufman (eds.), *The Politics of Economic Adjustment: International Constraints, Distributive Conflicts and the State* (pp. 139-181). Princeton N.J.: Princeton University Press.

Evans, Peter and John D. Stephens. 1988. "Studying Development since the Sixties: The Emergence of a New Comparative Political Economy," *Theory and Society* 17: 713-745.

Fernández-Kelly, Maria Patricia. 1983a. *For We Are Sold, I and My People: Women and Industry in Mexico's Frontier.* Albany: State University of New York Press.

———. 1983b. "Mexican Border Industrialization, Female Labor Force Participation and Migration," in Nash and Fernández-Kelly (eds.), *Women, Men and the International Division of Labor* (pp. 205-223). Albany: State University of New York Press.

———. 1987. "Technology and Employment along the U.S.–Mexican Border," in Carolyn Thorup (ed.), *The United States and Mexico: Face to Face with the New Technology.* New Brunswick: Transaction Books.

Fishlow, Albert. 1990. "The Latin American State," *Journal of Economic Perspectives* 4(3): 61-74.

Fitzgerald, E. V. K. 1985. "The Financial Constraint on Relative Autonomy: The State and Capital Accumulation in Mexico, 1940-82," in Christian Anglade and Carlos Fortin (eds.), *The State and Capital Accumulation in Latin America*. London: Macmillan Press.

Folbre, Nancy. 1986. "Cleaning House: New Perspectives on Households and Economic Development," *Journal of Development Economics* 22(1): 5-40.

Fowler Salamini, Heather. 1990. "Tamaulipas," in Thomas Benjamin and Mark Wasserman (eds.), *Provinces of the Revolution: Essays on Regional Mexican History, 1910-1929* (pp. 185-217). Albuquerque: University of New Mexico Press.

Fraad, H., S. Resnick, and R. Wolff. 1989. "For Every Knight in Shining Armor There's a Castle Waiting to Be Cleaned: A Marxist-Feminist Analysis of the Household. *Rethinking Marxism* 2(4): 10-69.

Frank, Andre Gunder. 1967. *Capitalism and Underdevelopment in Latin America*. New York: Modern Reader.

Froebel, F., J. Heinrichs, and O. Kreye. 1980. *The New International Division of Labor*. London: Cambridge University Press.

Fuentes, Annette and Barbara Ehrenreich. 1983. *Women in the Global Factory*. New York: Institute for New Communication.

Fuentes, Coronel Ignacio. 1974. "El Paso de Doña Cecilia," *Revista Tamaulipas*. 230: 83.

García Canclini, N. 1992. *Culturas Híbridas : Estrategias para Entrar y Salir de la Modernidad*. Buenos Aires: Editorial Sudamericana.

Gereffi, Gary. 1990. "Paths of Industrialization: An Overview," in Gary Gereffi and Donald Wyman (eds.), *Manufacturing Miracles: Paths of Industrialization in Latin America and East Asia* (pp. 3-31). Princeton, N.J.,: Princeton University Press.

Gereffi, Gary and Donald Wyman, eds. 1990. *Manufacturing Miracles: Paths of Industrialization in Latin America and East Asia*. Princeton: Princeton University Press.

Gibson-Graham, J. K. 1996. *The End of Capitalism (as we knew it): A Feminist Critique of Political Economy*. Cambridge, Mass.: Blackwell Publishers, Inc.

Gold, Thomas. 1986. *State and Society in Taiwan's Economic Miracle*. Armonk, N.Y.: Sharpe.

Gómez-Peña, G. 1996. *New World Border: Prophecies, Poems and Loqueras for the End of the Century*. San Francisco: City Lights Books.

González Casanova, Pablo and Hector Aguilar Camin. 1985. *Mexico ante la Crisis*. Mexico DF: Siglo Veintiuno Editores.

González de La Rocha, Mercedes and Agustin Escobar Latapi. eds. 1991. *Social Responses to Mexico's Economic Crisis*. San Diego: Center for U.S.-Mexican Studies.

Grayson, George W. 1980. *The Politics of Mexican Oil*. Pittsburgh: The University of Pittsburgh Press.

———. 1989. *The Mexican Labor Machine: Power, Politics and Patronage.* Washington D.C.: The Center for Strategic and International Studies.

Grossman, Rachael. 1979. "Women's Place in the Integrated Circuit," *Southeast Asia Chronicle* 66: 2-17.

Haber, Stephen H. 1989. *Industry and Underdevelopment: The Industrialization of Mexico, 1890-1940.* Stanford: Stanford University Press.

Haggard, Stephan. 1990. *Pathways from the Periphery: The Politics and Growth of the Newly Industrializing Countries.* Ithaca, N.Y.: Cornell University Press.

Haggard, Stephan and Tun-Jen Cheng. 1987. "State and Capital in East Asian NICs," in Frederic Deyo (ed.), *The Political Economy of the New Asian Industrialism* (pp. 84-135). Ithaca, N.Y.,: Cornell University Press.

Hamilton, Nora. 1982. *The Limits of State Autonomy: Postrevolutionary Mexico.* Princeton, N.J.: Princeton University Press.

———. 1986. "State-Class Alliances and Conflicts: Issues and Actors in the Mexican Economic Crisis," in Nora Hamilton and Timothy F. Harding (eds.), *Modern Mexico: State, Economy and Social Conflict* (pp. 148-174). Beverly Hills, Calif.: Sage Publications.

Harris, Olivia. 1981. "Households As Natural Units," in Kate Young, Carol Wolkowitz, and Roslyn Mccullagh (eds.), *Of Marriage and the Market: Women's Subordination Internationally and Its Lessons* (pp. 136-156). London: Routledge.

Hayford, A. 1974. "The Geography of Women: An Historical Introduction," *Antipode* 6(2): 1-19.

Hughes, Helen, ed. 1988. *Industrialization in East Asia.* Cambridge: Cambridge University Press.

Huxley, M. and H. P. M. Winchester. 1991. "Residential Differentiation and Social Reproduction: The Interrelations of Class, Gender and Space," *Environment and Planning D: Society and Space* 9(1): 233-240.

INEGI. 1985. *Estadística de la Industria Maquiladora de Exportación, 1975-1983.* Mexico, DF: Secretaria de Programación y Presupuesto.

———. 1990a. *Anuario de Estadísticas del Estado de Sonora. Edición 1990.*

———. 1990b. *Censo General de Población. Tamaulipas.*

Infante A., Eduardo. 1991. *Cronicas y Anecdotas de Ciudad Madero, Tamaulipas.* Ciudad Madero: N.P.

International Community Prospectus: Nogales, Arizona and Nogales, Sonora. 1977. Phoenix, Arizona Office of Economic Planning and Development.

Israel, Arturo. 1991. "The Changing Role of the State in Development: A Leaner, Specialized and More Effective Public Sector Is Needed to Support a Healthy Private Sector," *Finance and Development* 28: 41-3.

Jenkins, Rhys. 1988. "Latin American Industrialization and the New International Division of Labor," University of East Anglia, School of Development Studies, Discussion Paper #205.

——. 1991a. "The Political Economy of Industrialization: A Comparison of Latin American and East Asian Newly Industrializing Countries," *Development and Change* 22(2): 197-231.

——. 1991b. "Learning from the Gang: Are There Lessons for Latin America from East Asia?" *Bulletin of Latin American Research* 10(1): 37-54.

Johnson, Chalmers. 1982. *MITI and the Japanese Miracle*. Stanford: Stanford University Press.

Kamel, Rachael. 1990. *The Global Factory: Analysis and Action for a New Economic Era*. American Friends Service Committee. Philadelphia: Penn.: Omega Press.

Kaufman, Robert R. 1990. "How Societies Change Development Models or Keep Them: Reflections on the Latin American Experience in the 1930s and the Postwar World," in Gary Gereffi and Donald Wyman (eds.), *Manufacturing Miracles: Paths of Industrialization in Latin America and East Asia* (pp. 110-138). Princeton, N.J.,: Princeton University Press.

King, Timothy. 1970. *Mexico: Industrialization and Trade Policies since 1940*. London: Oxford University Press. Published for OECD.

Kitching, Gavin. 1982. *Development and Underdevelopment in Historical Perspective*. London: Routledge.

Knopp, Larry. 1989. "Gentrification and Gay Community Development in a New Orleans Neighborhood." Ph.D. thesis. Department of Geography, University of Iowa, Iowa City, Iowa.

——. 1990. "Some Theoretical Implications of Gay Involvement in an Urban Land Market," *Political Geography Quarterly* 9: 337-352.

——. 1992. "Sexuality and the Spatial Dynamics of Capitalism," *Environment and Planning D: Society and Space* 10(6): 651-670.

Kochan, Leslie. 1989. "The Maquiladoras and Toxics: The Hidden Costs of Production South of the Border," AFL-CIO Publication No. 186-PO690-5.

Kofman, Eleanore and Rosemary Sales 1996. The Geography of Gender and Welfare in Europe. in M. D. García-Ramon and J. Monk. (eds.), *Women of the European Union* (pp. 31-60). London, Routledge.

Koo, Hagen. 1984. "The Interplay of State, Social Class, and World System in East Asian Development: The Cases of South Korea and Taiwan," in Frederic Deyo (ed.), *The Political Economy of the New Asian Industrialization* (pp. 165-181). Ithaca: Cornell University Press.

Kopinak, Kathyrn. 1996. *Desert Capitalism: Maquiladoras in North America's Western Industrial Corridor*. Tucson: University of Arizona Press.

Krueger, Anne. 1974. "The Political Economy of the Rent-Seeking Society," *American Economic Review* (64): 291-303.

——. 1990. "Government Failures in Development," *Journal of Economic Perspectives* 4(3): 12.

La Botz, Dan. 1992. *Mask of Democracy: Labor Suppression in Mexico Today*. Boston: South End Press.

Lamphere, L. 1987. *From Working Daughters to Working Mothers: Immigrant Women in a New England Industrial Community.* Ithaca: Cornell University Press.

Lancaster Regionalism Group. 1985. *Localities, Class and Gender.* London: Pion.

Lara Enriquez, Blanca Esthela. 1990. "Tecnología Flexibilidad en el Trabajo Nuevo Reto para los Trabajadores," en F. Mora and V. M. Reynosos (coords.), *Modernización y Legislación Laboral en el Noroeste de México.* El Colegio de Sonora. Fundación Friedrich Ebert. Hermosillo.

Laslett, Barbara and Joanna Brenner. 1989. "Gender and Social Reproduction: Historical Perspectives," *Annual Review of Sociology* 15: 381-404.

Lauria, M. and L. Knopp. 1985. "Towards an Analysis of the Role of the Gay Community in the Urban Renaissance," *Urban Geography* 6(2): 152-169.

Lee, Chung H. 1992. "The Government, Financial System, and Large Private Enterprises in Economic Development of South Korea," *World Development* 20: 187-197.

Lewis, Jane. 1984. "The Role of Female Employment in the Industrial Restructuring and Regional Development of the United Kingdom," *Antipode* 16(3): 47-60.

Ley del Seguro Social y su Reglamento. 1992. México.

Ley Federal de Trabajo. 1992. México.

Linder, Marc and Ingrid Nygaard 1998. *Void Where Prohibited: Rest Breaks and the Right to Urinate on Company Time.* Ithaca, N.Y.: ILR Press.

Lipietz, Alain. 1987. *Miracles and Mirages: The Crises of Global Fordism.* London: Verso.

Los Municipios de Tamaulipas. 1988. *Coleccion: Enciclopedia de los Municipios de Mexico.* México: Secretaria de Gobernación y Gobierno.

Lustig, Nora. 1993. "NAFTA: A Mexican Perspective," *SAIS Review* 13(1): 57-67.

McDowell, Linda and Doreen Massey. 1984. "A Woman's Place?" in Doreen Massey and John Allen (eds.), *Geography Matters!* (pp. 128-147). Cambridge: Cambridge University Press.

Mackenzie, Suzanne. 1986. "Women's Responses to Economic Restructuring: Changing Gender, Changing Space," in Hamilton R. And M. Barrett (eds.), *The Politics of Diversity,* (pp. 81-100). London: Verso.

———. 1989. "Women in the City," in Richard Peet and Nigel Thrift (eds.), *New Models in Geography* (pp. 109-126). London: Unwin Hyman.

Mackenzie, Suzanne and Damaris Rose. 1983. "Industrial Change, the Domestic Economy and Home Life," in J. Anderson, S. Duncan, and R. Hudson (eds.), *Redundant Spaces in Cities and Regions?* (pp. 155-200). London: Academic Press.

Mackintosh, Maureen. 1981. "Gender and Economics: The Sexual Division of Labor and the Subordination of Women," in Kate Young, Carol Wolkowitz, and Roslyn McCullagh (eds.), *Of Marriage and the Market: Women's Subordination Internationally and Its Lessons* (pp. 3-17). London: Routledge.

Massey, Doreen. 1984. *Spatial Divisions of Labor: Social Processes and the Geography of Production Systems*. London: Macmillan.

Maxfield, Sylvia. 1990. *Governing Capital: International Finance and Mexican Politics*. Ithaca: Cornell University Press.

Merriam, Sharan B. 1988. *Case Study Research in Education: A Qualitative Approach*. San Francisco: Jossey-Bass Publishers.

Meyer, Michael C. and William L. Sherman. 1991. *The Course of Mexican History*, 4th ed. Oxford: Oxford University Press.

Middlebrook, Kevin, ed. 1991. *Unions, Workers and the State in Mexico*. San Diego: Center for U.S.-Mexican Studies.

Middlebrook, Kevin. 1995. *The Paradox of Revolution: Labor, the State, and Authoritariasm in Mexico*. Baltimore: The Johns Hopkins University Press.

Middleton, Philip Harvey. 1919. *Industrial Mexico; 1919 facts and figures*. New York, Dodd, Mead and company.

Momsen, Janet and Janet Townsend, eds. 1987. *Geography of Gender in the Third World*. London: State University of New York Press.

Mosk, Sanford A. 1950. *Industrial Revolution in Mexico*. Berkeley: University of California Press.

Munck, Ronald. 1988. *The New International Labour Studies: An Introduction*. London: Zed Books.

O'Donnell, Guillermo. 1978. "Reflections on the Pattern of Change in the Bureaucratic Authoritarian State," *Latin American Research Review* 13(1): 1-38.

Ong, Aihwa. 1985. "Industrialization and Prostitution in Southeast Asia," *Southeast Asia Chronicle* 96: 2-6.

———. 1987. *Spirits of Resistance and Capitalist Discipline: Factory Women in Malaysia*. Albany: State University of New York Press.

Onis, Zija. 1991. "The Logic of the Developmental State," *Comparative Politics* 24: 109-26.

Orantes, Lilia. 1987. "La Industria Maquiladora y su Impacto sobre la Fuerza de Trabajo: El Caso de Nogales, 1960-1986." Tésis del Departamento de Ciencias Sociales, Universidad de Sonora, Hermosillo.

Palma, Gabriel. 1978. "Dependency: A Formal Theory of Underdevelopment or a Methodology for the Analysis of Concrete Situations of Underdevelopment?" *World Development* 6: 881-924.

Pardo-Maurer, R. and J. Rodríguez 1992. *Access Mexico: Emerging Market Handbook and Directory: 1992-1993 edition*. Arlington, Va.: Cambridge Data and Development.

Peck, J. A. 1992. "Invisible Threads: Homeworking, Labour-Market Relations, and Industrial Restructuring in the Australian Clothing Trade," *Environment and Planning D: Society and Space* 10(6): 671-690.

Peet, Richard. 1987. "Industrial Devolution, Underconsumption and the Third World Crisis," *World Development* 15(6): 777-788.

Peña, Devon. 1987. "Tortuosidad: Shop Floor Struggles of Female Maquiladora Workers," in Vicki Ruiz and Susan Tiano (eds.), *Women on the U.S.-Mexico Border: Responses to Change* (pp. 129-154). Boston and London: Allen and Unwin.

Perlo Cohen, Manuel. 1987. "Exploring the Spatial Effects of the Internationalization of the Mexican Economy," in Manuel Castells and Jeffery Henderson (eds.), *Global Restructuring and Territorial Development*. London: Sage.

Petras, James and Dennis Engbarth. 1986. "Third World Industrialization: Implications for Trade Union Struggles," in James Petras (ed.), *Latin America: Bankers, Generals and the Struggle for Social Justice*. Totowa, N.J.: Rowman & Littlefield.

Pratt, Geraldine. 1993. "Reflections on Poststructuralism and Feminist Empirics, Theory and Practice," *Antipode* 25(1): 51-63.

Pratt, Geraldine and Susan Hanson. 1988. "Gender, Class and Space," *Environment and Planning D: Society and Space* 6(1): 15-36.

———. 1991a. "On Theoretical Subtlety, Gender, Class and Space: A Reply to Huxley and Winchester," *Environment and Planning D: Society and Space* 9(1): 241-246.

———. 1991b. "On the Links between Home and Work: Family-Household Strategies in a Buoyant Labour Market," *International Journal of Urban and Regional Research* 15: 55-74.

Pryer, J. 1987. "Production and Reproduction of Malnutrition in an Urban Slum in Khulna Bangladesh," in J. Momsen and J. Townsend (eds.), *Geography and Gender in the Third World* (pp. 131-149). London, Hutchinson.

Ramírez, Jose Carlos. 1988. "La Nueva Industria Sonorense: El Caso de las Maquilas de Exportación," en Jose Carlos Ramírez (ed.), *La Nueva Industrialización En Sonora: El Caso de los Sectores de Alta Tecnología* (pp. 5-119). Hermosillo: El Colegio de Sonora.

Ramírez, Miguel. 1989. *Mexico's Economic Crisis: Its Origins and Consequences*. New York: Praeger.

Randall, Laura. 1989. *The Political Economy of Mexican Oil*. New York: Praeger.

Ros, Jaime. 1992. "Free Trade Area or Common Capital Area? Notes on Mexico-U.S. Economic Integration and Current NAFTA Negotiations," *Journal of Interamerican Studies and World Affairs* 34(2): 53-91.

Rowbotham, S. 1973. *Hidden from History: 300 Years of Women's Oppression and the Fight against It*. London: Pluto Press.

Roxborough, Ian. 1984. *Unions and Politics in Mexico: The Case of the Automobile Industry*. Cambridge: Cambridge University Press.

Ruiz, Ramon Eduardo. 1988. *The People of Sonora and the Yankee Capitalists*. Tucson: The University of Arizona Press.

Safa, Helen I. 1981. "Runaway Shops and Female Employment: The Search for Cheap Labor," *Signs* 7(2): 418-33.

———. 1990. "Women and Industrialization in the Caribbean," in Sharon Stichter and Jane L. Parpart (eds.), *Women, Employment and the Family in the International Division of Labor*. London: Macmillan.

Sage, Colin. 1993. "Deconstructing the Household: Women's Roles under Commodity Relations in Highland Bolivia," in Janet H. Momsen and Vivian Kinnaird (eds.), *Different Places, Different Voices* (pp. 243-255). London: Routledge.

Salaff, Janet W. 1981. *Working Daughters of Hong Kong: Filial Piety or Power in the Family?* Cambridge: Cambridge University Press.

———. 1990. "Women, the Family and the State: Hong Kong, Taiwan, Singapore– Newly Industrialized Countries in Asia," in Sharon Stichter and Jane L. Parpart (eds.), *Women, Employment and the Family in the International Division of Labor* (pp. 98-136). London: Macmillan.

Sánchez, Roberto. 1990a. "Condiciones de Vida de los Trabajadores de la Maquiladora en Tijuana y Nogales," *Frontera Norte* 2(4): 153-181.

———. 1990b. "Health and Environmental Risks of the Maquiladora in Mexicali," *Natural Resources Journal* 30 (Winter): 163-186.

Sanderson, Steven E. 1992. *The Politics of Trade in Latin American Development*. Stanford: Stanford University Press.

Schmink, Marianne. 1984. "Household Economic Strategies: A Review and Research Agenda," *Latin American Research Review* 19(3): 87-101.

Schwartz, Scott. 1987. "The Border Industrialization Program of Mexico," *Southwest Journal of Business and Economics* 4: 1-51.

Scott, Allen. 1986. "The Semiconductor Industry in Southeast Asia: Organization, Location and International Division of Labor." Los Angeles: UCLA, Institute for Industrial Relations. Working Paper #101.

Sekula, Allan. 1997. *Dead Letter Office*. Nederlands Foto Instituut. Rotterdam.

Shapiro, Helen and Lance Taylor. 1990. "The State and Industrial Strategy," *World Development* 18: 861-878.

Silattum. 1974. "Como era Dona Cecilia, antes se ser Declarado Municipo Libre," *Revista Tamaulipas* 231: 28-34.

Sklair, Leslie. 1989. *Assembling for Development: The Maquila Industry in Mexico and the United States*. Boston: Unwin Hyman.

Smith, Joan and Immanuel Wallerstein. 1984. *Household and the World Economy*. Beverly Hills: Sage.

———. 1992. *Creating and Transforming Households: The Constraints of the World-Economy*. Cambridge: Cambridge University Press.

Spalding, Rose J. 1981. "State Power and Its Limits: Corporatism in Mexico," *Comparative Political Studies* 14(2): 139-161.

Spero, Joan Edelman. 1990. *The Politics of International Economic Relations*. Fourth ed. New York: St. Martin's Press.

Staudt, Kathleen. 1986. "Economic Change and Ideological Lag in Households of Maquila Workers in Ciudad Juarez," in Gay Young (ed.), *The Social Ecology and Economic Development of Ciudad Juárez*. Boulder, Colo.: Westview Press.

Stichter, Sharon. 1990. "Women, Employment and the Family: Current Debates," in Sharon Stichter and Jane Parpart (eds.), *Women, Employment and the Family in the International Division of Labor* (pp. 11-71). Philadelphia: Temple University Press.

Story, Dale. 1986. *Industry, the State and Public Policy in Mexico*. Austin: University of Texas Press.

Teichman, Judith A. 1988. *Policymaking in Mexico: From Boom to Crisis*. Boston: Allen and Unwin.

Trujillo Y Nunez, Armando. 1974. "Dona Cecilia, Un Nombre que se Trago el Olvido," *Revista Tamaulipas* 230: 16-25.

Thompson, Lanny. 1992. "Mexico," in Smith, Joan and Immanuel Wallerstein (eds.), *Creating and Transforming Households: The Constraints of the World Economy* (pp. 145-186). Beverly Hills: Sage.

Thrift, Nigel. 1988. "The Geography of Finance Capital," in Manuel Castells and Jeffery Henderson (eds.), *Global Restructuring and Territorial Development* (pp. 203-233). London: Sage.

Tiano, Susan. 1987. "Women's Work and Unemployment in Northern Mexico," in Vicki Ruiz and Susan Tiano (eds.), *Women on the U.S.-Mexico Border: Responses to Change* (pp. 17-40). Boston: Allen and Unwin.

———. 1990. "Maquiladora Women: A New Category of Workers?" in Kathyrn Ward (ed.), *Women Workers and Global Restructuring*. Ithaca: ILR Press, Cornell University.

Trujillo y Núñez, Armando. 1974. "Doña Cecilia: Un Nombre Que se Trago el Olvido," *Revista Tamaulipas* 230: 16-25.

Twin Plant News. 1990. "The ABCs of Mexican Labor Relations." (May): 40-43, 65.

U.S. Congress. 1993. *U.S.-Mexico Trade: Pulling Together or Pulling Apart?* Washington, D.C.: U.S. Government Printing Office.

Van Waas, Michael. 1981. "The Multinationals' Strategy for Labor: Foreign Assembly Plants in Mexico's Border Industrialization Program." Ph.D. dissertation. Stanford University.

Villarreal, René. 1990. "The Latin American Strategy of Import Substitution: Failure or Paradigm for the Region?" in Gary Gereffi and Donald Wyman (eds.), *Manufacturing Miracles: Paths of Industrialization in Latin America and East Asia* (pp. 292-320). Princeton: Princeton University Press.

Wade, Robert. 1989. "What Economics Can Learn from East Asian Success," *Annals of the American Academy of Political and Social Science* 505: 68-79.

———. 1990a. "Industrial Policy in East Asia: Does It Lead or Follow the Market," in Gary Gereffi and Donald Wyman (eds.), *Manufacturing Miracles: Paths of*

Industrialization in Latin America and East Asia (pp. 231-266). Princeton: Princeton University Press.

———. 1990b. *Governing the Market: Economic Theory and the Role of Government in East Asian Industrialization.* Princeton: Princeton University Press.

———. 1992. "State and Market Revisited," *The Economist* 323: 81.

Walby, Sylvia. 1994. "Methodological and Theoretical Issues in the Comparative Analysis of Gender Relations in Western Europe." *Environment and Planning A* 26(9): 1339-1354.

Walby, S. and P. Bagguley. 1989. "Gender Restructuring: Five Labour Markets Compared," *Environment and Planning D: Society and Space* 7(3): 277-292.

Ward, Kathyrn, ed. 1990. *Women Workers and Global Restructuring.* Ithaca: ILR Press, Cornell University.

Ward, Peter. 1986. *Welfare Politics in Mexico: Papering Over the Cracks.* London: Allen and Unwin.

Warren, Bill. 1973. "Imperialism and Capitalist Industrialization," *New Left Review* 81: 3-44.

Weisman, Alan. 1986. *La Frontera: The United States Border with Mexico.* Tucson: The University of Arizona Press.

Whitehead, Annie. 1981. "'I'm Hungry, Mum': The Politics of Domestic Budgeting," in Kate Young, Carol Wolkowitz, and Roslyn McCullagh (eds.), *Of Marriage and the Market: Women's Subordination Internationally and Its Lessons* (pp. 93-116). London: Routledge.

Williams, E. J. and J. T. Passé-Smith 1992. *The Unionization of the Maquiladora Industry : the Tamaulipan Case in National Context.* San Diego, Calif. : Institute for Regional Studies of the Californias, San Diego State University.

Wolf, Diane L. 1990. "Linking Women's Labor with the Global Economy: Factory Workers and Their Families in Rural Java," in Kathyrn Ward (ed.), *Women Workers and Global Restructuring.* Ithaca: ILR Press, Cornell University.

Womack, John, Jr. 1978. "The Mexican Economy during the Revolution, 1910-1920: Historiography and Analysis," *Marxist Perspectives.* (Winter): 80-123.

——— 1979. "The Historiography of Mexican Labor," in *El Trabajo y los Trabajadores en la Historia de Mexico* (pp. 739-756). Mexico City and Tucson: University of Arizona Press.

Women in Geography Study Group of the Institute of British Geographers. 1986. *Geography and Gender: An Introduction to Feminist Geography.* London: Hutchinson.

Wood, Stephen, ed. 1989. *The Transformation of Work.* London: Unwin Hyman.

World Bank. 1988. *Korea's Experience with the Development of Trade and Industry.* Washington: Economic Development Institute of the World Bank.

Young, Gay and Susan Christopherson. 1986. "Household Structure and Activity in Ciudad Juárez," in Gay Young (ed.), *The Social Ecology and Economic Development of Ciudad Juárez* (pp. 65-95). Boulder, Colo.: Westview Press.

Newspaper Sources

Arizona Daily Star

November 1, 1967. "Motorola Inc. Opens New Nogales, Sonora Plant."
June 30, 1970. "Parque Industrial de Nogales Dedicated: Ground Broken for Mexican Plant of Lear Jet Stereo."
July 1, 1970. Ready, Alma. "Nogales Industry Park Dedicated: Sonorans Hail U.S. Cooperation."
September 12, 1971. "New Buildings Elbowing the Old in Nogales as Area Economy Booms."
November 15, 1971. (Cited in Orantes 1987, p. 21)
May 5, 1975. "Industry Boom a Hardship in Sonora Town."
May 5, 1975. "Recession, Wages Force Plants to Leave."
December 17, 1976. "President Carter Asks for Aid to Border Cities."
April 2, 1982. "Work Stoppages Protest Devalued Peso Wages."
April 13, 1982. "Border Peso Pinch."
May 19, 1982. "Señor Ricardo Clothing Factory Closes."
June 20, 1982. Panzarella, Ray. "Lean Times Put Squeeze on Border Plants."
June 17, 1983. "Border Cities Are Still Struggling after Peso Devaluation."
June 9, 19985. "Leaderless Squatters in Nogales, Sonora are Planning to Stay."
January 19, 1986. Maish, James H. "Squatters Covet Medium under Message."
June 15, 1986. Maish, James H. "Nogales Sonora Squatter Camp Tense."
March 1, 1987. Turner, Mark Holman. "Tuesday Vote May Give Arizona Border Its First Unionized Twin Plant."
March 2, 1987. "Strike Shuts Down Hermosillo Ford Plant."
March 4, 1987. Turner, Mark Holman. "Nogales Twin Plant Worker Reject UAW Organizing Effort."
March 12, 1987. "Strike–Hermosillo Ford Plant."
October 4, 1987. Svejcara, Bob. "Dad, Son Share Twin Plant Goal: Both Travel Nation Selling 'Shelter' Plan."
July 4, 1988. Roderick, Gary. "Jobs Lost, Jobs Gained."
July 9, 1988. "Chrysler to Close Operation at Coleman Products in 1989, Causing Loss of 250 Jobs."
February 12, 1989. "Nogales Builds Diverse Economy."

Arizona Republic

June 22, 1969. "Motorola Plant U.S.-Mexico Link."
October 17, 1971. Malone, Frank. "The Greening of the Border."

April 18, 1989. Kramer, Jerry. "Weak Unions Offer a Labor Paradise across the Border."

Nogales International

December 26, 1974. "500 Let Go by Motorola Across Border."
March 27, 1975. "'Serious' Twin Plant Problem Reported."
April 10, 1975. "Problems of Twin Plants Deepening."
April 17, 1975. "Plant Slowdown Expected to End."
May 26, 1976. "'Twin Plants' Plight Improves; Not Slipping nor Stagnating."
April 14, 1982. Soto, Teresa. "Some Mexicans Get Pay Hikes."
May 22, 1982. Soto, Teresa. "Economy stalls development on the Border."

Tucson Citizen

September 13, 1971. "$15 Million Now in 'Twin Plants.'"

Wall Street Journal

May 25, 1976, p. 22.

Index

About the Author

A former active member of the International Brotherhood of Electrical Workers and construction electrician, Altha J. Cravey earned a doctorate from the University of Iowa where she was a recipient of the Iowa Fellowship. Currently Assistant Professor of Geography at the University of North Carolina at Chapel Hill, her research centers on labor and gender in contemporary Mexico.